International Labour and Employment Compliance Handbook

www.kluwerlawonline.com

Labour and Employment Compliance in Australia

International Bar Association

Labour and Employment Compliance in Australia

Seventh Edition

John Tuck

Stephen Price

Jack de Flamingh

Nick Le Mare

This publication is part of the International Labour and Employment Compliance Handbook, available on www.kluwerlawonline.com

Editors: Salvador del Rey and Robert J. Mignin
Associate Editor: Juan Bonilla

the global voice of
the legal profession

Wolters Kluwer

Published by:
Kluwer Law International B.V.
PO Box 316
2400 AH Alphen aan den Rijn
The Netherlands
E-mail: lrs-sales@wolterskluwer.com
Website: www.wolterskluwer.com/en/solutions/kluwerlawinternational

Sold and distributed by:
Wolters Kluwer Legal & Regulatory U.S.
920 Links Avenue
Landisville, PA 17538
United States of America
E-mail: customer.service@wolterskluwer.com

ISBN 978-94-035-3797-9

e-Book: ISBN 978-94-035-3807-5
web-PDF: ISBN 978-94-035-3817-4

All listed titles are also available on lrus.wolterskluwer.com

1. Argentina: Julio César Stefanoni Zani & Enrique Alfredo Betemps, *Labour and Employment Compliance in Argentina, 11th edition*, 2023 (ISBN 978-94-035-1857-2)
2. Australia: John Tuck, Stephen Price, Jack de Flamingh & Nick Le Mare *Labour and Employment Compliance in Australia, 7th edition*, 2023 (ISBN 978-94-035-379-79)
3. Belgium: Chris Van Olmen, *Labour and Employment Compliance in Belgium, 8th edition*, 2023 (ISBN 978-94-035-2197-8)
4. Brazil: Rodrigo Seizo Takano, Andrea Giamondo Massei & Murilo Caldeira Germiniani, *Labour and Employment Compliance in Brazil, 10th edition*, 2023 (ISBN 978-94-035-1897-8)
5. Canada: Kevin Coon, *Labour and Employment Compliance in Canada, 3rd edition*, 2023 (ISBN 978-90-411-9339-1)
6. Chile: Gerardo Otero A., María Dolores Echeverría F., & Javier Sabido, *Labour and Employment Compliance in Chile, 11th edition*, 2023 (ISBN 978-94-035-1987-6)
7. China: King & Wood Mallesons, *Labour and Employment Compliance in China, 6th edition*, 2021 (ISBN 978-94-035-3894-5)
8. France: Pascale Lagesse, *Labour and Employment Compliance in France, 11th edition*, 2023 (ISBN 978-94-035-2137-4)
9. Germany: Gerlind Wisskirchen & Martin Lützeler, *Labour and Employment Compliance in Germany, 11th edition*, 2023 (ISBN 978-94-035-2347-7)
10. India: Manishi Pathak, *Labour and Employment Compliance in India, 11th edition*, 2023 (ISBN 978-94-035-1927-2)
11. Ireland: Duncan Inverarity & Tríona Sugrue, *Labour and Employment Compliance in Ireland, 10th edition*, 2023 (ISBN 978-94-035-2227-2)
12. Israel: Pnina Broder-Manor & Ilan Winder, *Labour and Employment Compliance in Israel, 10th edition*, 2023 (ISBN 978-94-035-2017-1)
13. Italy: Angelo Zambelli, *Labour and Employment Compliance in Italy, 11th edition*, 2023 (ISBN 978-94-035-1957-9)
14. Japan: Yoshikazu Sugino, *Labour and Employment Compliance in Japan, 11th edition*, 2023 (ISBN 978-94-035-1827-5)
15. Republic of Korea: Sang Wook Cho, Soojung Lee, Christopher Mandel & Tae Eun Lee, *Labour and Employment Compliance in the Republic of Korea, 9th edition*, 2023 (ISBN 978-94-035-2167-1)
16. Mexico: Oscar De La Vega Gómez, *Labour and Employment Compliance in Mexico, 11th edition*, 2023 (ISBN 978-94-035-2377-4)
17. The Netherlands: Els de Wind & Cara Pronk, *Labour and Employment Compliance in the Netherlands, 5th edition*, 2022 (ISBN 978-94-035-1594-6)
18. Poland: Barbara Jóźwik, *Labour and Employment Compliance in Poland, 11th edition*, 2023 (ISBN 978-94-035-2407-8)
19. Russia: Anna-Stefaniya Chepik, *Labour and Employment Compliance in Russia*, 2013 (ISBN 978-90-411-4925-1)

20. Saudi Arabia: Sara Khoja & Sarit Thomas, *Labour and Employment Compliance in Saudi Arabia, 6th edition*, 2023 (ISBN 978-94-035-2107-7)
21. South Africa: Susan Stelzner†, Stuart Harrison, Brian Patterson & Zahida Ebrahim, *Labour and Employment Compliance in South Africa, 11th edition*, 2023 (ISBN 978-94-035-2257-9)
22. Spain: Salvador del Rey & Ana Campos, *Labour and Employment Compliance in Spain, 11th edition*, 2023 (978-94-035-2077-3)
23. Turkey: Elif Nur Çakır Vurgun, Gökhan Akçaalan, Özgür Kızıltan & Zeynep Adıyaman, *Labour and Employment Compliance in Turkey, 9th edition*, 2023 (ISBN 978-94-035-2287-6)
24. United Arab Emirates: Sara Khoja & Sarit Thomas, *Labour and Employment Compliance in the United Arab Emirates, 10th edition*, 2023 (ISBN 978-94-035-2047-6)
25. United Kingdom: Ed Mills, Ailie Murray, Anna West, Gareth Walls & Olivia Boyle, *Labour and Employment Compliance in The United Kingdom, 4th edition*, 2023 (ISBN 978-94-035-2317-0)
26. United States: Andrew J. Boling, Robert J. Mignin, Madeline F. Kelleher & David M. Serwer, *Labour and Employment Compliance in the United States, 8th edition*, 2023 (ISBN 978-94-035-1736-0)

International Bar Association
The Global Voice of the Legal Profession

The International Bar Association (IBA), established in 1947, is the world's leading organization of international legal practitioners, bar associations and law societies. The IBA influences the development of international law reform and shapes the future of the legal profession throughout the world. It has a membership of over 40,000 individual lawyers and almost 200 bar associations and law societies spanning all continents. It has considerable expertise in providing assistance to the global legal community.

Grouped into two divisions – the Legal Practice Division and the Public and Professional Interest Division – the IBA covers all practice areas and professional interests, providing members with access to leading experts and up-to-date information. Through the various committees of the divisions, the IBA enables an interchange of information and views among its members as to laws, practices and professional responsibilities relating to the practice of business law around the globe. Additionally, the IBA's high-quality publications and world-class conferences provide unrivalled professional development and network-building opportunities for international legal practitioners and professional associates.

The IBA's Bar Issues Commission provides an invaluable forum for IBA member organisations to discuss all matters relating to law at an international level.

The IBA's Human Rights Institute (IBAHRI) works across the Association, to promote, protect and enforce human rights under a just rule of law, and to preserve the independence of the judiciary and the legal profession worldwide.

Other institutions established by the IBA include the Southern Africa Litigation Centre and the International Legal Assistance Consortium.

Employment and Industrial Relations Law Committee

The aims of the committee are to develop and exchange knowledge of employment and industrial relations law and practice. Members support each other through the provision of innovative ideas and practical assistance on day-to-day issues. In addition, through its journal and through presentations, conferences, the committee ensures the dissemination of up-to-date law and practice in this highly important business area.

INTERNATIONAL BAR ASSOCIATION

International Bar Association Global Employment Institute

The IBA Global Employment Institute (IBA GEI) was formed in early 2010 for the purpose of developing for multinationals and worldwide institutions a global and strategic approach to the key legal issues in the human resources and human capital fields.

Drawing on the resources and expertise of the IBA membership, the IBA GEI will provide a unique contribution in the field of employment, discrimination and immigration law, on a diverse range of global issues, to private and public organizations throughout the world. The IBA GEI is designed to enhance the management, performance and productivity of these organizations and help achieve best practice in their human capital and management functions from a strategic perspective.

The IBA GEI will become the leading voice and authority on global HR issues by virtue of having a number of the world's leading labour and employment practitioners in its ranks, and the support and resource of the world's largest association of international lawyers.

Further information

International Bar Association, 4th Floor, 10 St Bride Street, London EC4A 4AD, United Kingdom, Tel: +44 (0)20 7842 0090, Fax: +44 (0)20 7842 0091, E-mail: member@int-bar.org, www.ibanet.org

About the International Labour and Employment Compliance Handbook

From 1976 through 1988, the International Bar Association and Kluwer Law International published the groundbreaking International Handbook on Contracts of Employment. This Handbook provided one of the first global overviews of the law of the international employment relationship.

Since publishing the first edition, globalization of business has created an increased demand for knowledge of labor and employment laws throughout the world. Therefore, along with Kluwer, we decided to publish an updated Handbook which we have titled the International Labour and Employment Compliance Handbook.

This new Handbook was intended to be a practical guide by providing a general overview of key labor and employment issues in multiple jurisdictions. Each chapter was written so that it is easy to understand by lawyers and non-lawyers alike. Each country author has also followed a standard outline to assist readers in analysing employment issues in each country.

The first edition of this new Handbook included nineteen (19) different countries.

This Handbook would not have been possible without the help and assistance of many people. Most importantly, the individual country authors are all distinguished legal practitioners who spent considerable time drafting and revising their country reports to meet difficult deadlines. We thank each of them. Our friends at Kluwer, especially Ewa Szkatula, have done a wonderful job in keeping the editors and the authors on schedule. Finally, we want to also express our gratitude to Cuatrecasas, Gonçalves Pereira, and Baker & McKenzie LLP for their valuable assistance in the coordination and organization of this project. Our warmest thanks to each of them.

Because of the success of the Handbook,Wolters Kluwer Law & Business decided to publish each country report also as a separate book to give a choice in obtaining the information. We hope this new format will be a helpful and useful resource just like the Handbook. Both formats are available in print and online.

The Editors

Salvador del Rey Guanter
Robert J. Mignin

March 2013

Table of Contents

Authors ix

Legal Compliance in Australia 1

1. Legal Framework: Employment Laws 1

2. Contracts of Employment 2
2.1. Overview 2
2.2. Written and Oral Employment Contracts 3
2.3. Employee Handbooks 4
2.4. Job Descriptions 4
2.5. Offer Letters 5
2.6. Checklist of Dos and Don'ts 5

3. Recruiting, Interviewing, Screening and Hiring Employees 5
3.1. Overview 5
3.2. Recruiting 6
3.3. Employment Applications 6
3.4. Pre-employment Enquiries 6
3.5. Pre-employment Tests and Examinations 7
3.6. Background, Reference and Credit Checks 7
3.7. Interviewing 8
3.8. Hiring Procedures 8
3.9. Fines and Penalties 8
3.10. Checklist of Dos and Don'ts 9

4. Managing Performance/Conduct 9
4.1. Overview 9
4.2. Coaching and Counselling 9
4.3. Written Evaluations 10
4.4. Warnings and Suspensions 10
4.5. Checklist of Dos and Don'ts 12

5. Termination of Employees for Performance or Disciplinary Reasons 12
5.1. Overview 12
5.2. Separation/Severance Pay 12
5.3. Fines and Penalties 13
5.4. Checklist of Dos and Don'ts 15

6. Layoffs, Reductions in Force and/or Redundancies as a Result of Job Eliminations or Other Restructuring 16
6.1. Overview 16
6.2. Reductions in Force/Layoffs/Job Eliminations 16
6.2.1. Genuine Redundancy Exclusion from Unfair Dismissal Claims 16
6.2.2. Information and Consultation Requirements about Major Workplace Changes in Modern Awards and Enterprise Agreements 17
6.2.3. FW Act Information and Consultation Requirements 17
6.2.4. Severance Pay 18
6.3. Fines and Penalties 19
6.4. Checklist of Dos and Don'ts 20

7. Labour and Employment Law Ramifications upon Acquisition or Sale of a Business 21
7.1. Overview 21
7.2. Acquisition of a Business 21
7.3. Acquisition Checklist 22
7.4. Sale of a Business 23
7.5. Sale Checklist 23

8. Use of Alternative Workforces: Independent Contractors, Contract Employees and Temporary or Leased Workers 24
8.1. Overview 24
8.2. Independent Contractors 24
8.2.1. Definition 24
8.2.2. Creating the Relationship 25
8.2.3. Compensation 25
8.2.4. Other Terms and Conditions 25
8.3. Contract Workers 25
8.3.1. Definition 25
8.3.2. No Obligation to Provide Salary, Wages and Benefits 26
8.3.3. No Right to Continued Work 26

8.4. Leased Workers 26
8.5. Checklist of Dos and Don'ts 27

9. Obligation to Bargain Collectively with Trade Unions: Employees' Right to Strike and a Company's Right to Continue Business Operations 27
9.1. Overview of Unions' Right to Organize 27
9.2. Right of Employees to Join Unions and Overview of Collective Bargaining Framework 28
9.3. How Employees Select Unions 29
9.4. Pre-election Campaigning 29
9.5. Multi-employer Bargaining 30
9.6. Unfair Labour Practices/GFB Obligations 31
9.7. Relocation of Work/Shutdown of Business 32
9.8. Checklist of Dos and Don'ts 33

10. Working Conditions: Hours of Work and Payment of Wages – By Statute or Collective Agreement 33
10.1. Overview of Wages and Hour Laws in Australia 33
10.2. Minimum Wage 34
10.3. Overtime 34
10.4. Meal and Rest Periods 35
10.5. Deductions from Wages 35
10.6. Garnishment 36
10.7. Exemptions to Wage and Hour Laws 36
10.8. Child Labour 37
10.9. Record-Keeping Requirements 38
10.9.1. Information That Must Be Maintained 38
10.9.2. Records That Must Be Retained 39
10.9.3. Failure to Maintain Required Records 40
10.10. Reductions in Compensation Caused by Economic Downturn 40
10.11. Checklist Dos and Don'ts 40

11. Other Working Conditions and Benefits: By Statute, Collective Agreements or Company Policy 41
11.1. Introduction 41
11.2. National Employment Standards 41
11.2.1. Right to Request Flexible Working Arrangements 41
11.2.2. Right to Request Casual Conversion 42
11.2.3. Parental Leave 42
11.2.4. Annual Leave 43
11.2.5. Personal Carer's Leave and Compassionate Leave 43

	11.2.6.	Community Service Leave	44
	11.2.7.	Long Service Leave	44
	11.2.8.	Public Holidays	44
	11.2.9.	Notice of Termination	45
		11.2.9.1. Redundancy Pay	45
11.3.	Modern Awards		45
11.4.	Collective Agreements		46
11.5.	Enforcement of the NES, Modern Awards and Collective Agreements		47
11.6.	General Protections		47
11.7.	Other Statutory Benefits		49
11.8.	Company Policies		50
11.9.	Checklist of Dos and Don'ts		51
12.	**Employee Benefits**		51
12.1.	Overview		51
12.2.	Compensation for Injured Employees		52
12.3.	Checklist of Dos and Don'ts		54
13.	**Company's Obligation to Provide a Safe and Healthy Workplace**		55
13.1.	Overview of Safety and Environmental Laws and Regulations		55
13.2.	Requirements		58
13.3.	Rights of Workers		59
13.4.	Rights of Employers		60
13.5.	Injury or Accident at Work		60
13.6.	Workplace Violence		61
13.7.	Fines and Penalties		61
13.8.	Checklists of Dos and Don'ts		62
14.	**Immigration, Secondment and Foreign Assignment**		62
14.1.	Overview		62
14.2.	Secondment/Foreign Assignment		63
14.3.	Checklist of Dos and Don'ts		63
15.	**Restrictive Covenants and Protection of Trade Secrets and Confidential Information**		63
15.1.	Overview		63
15.2.	Restrictive Covenants and Non-compete Agreements		65
15.3.	Checklist of Dos and Don'ts		67
16.	**Protection of Whistle-Blowing Claims**		67
16.1.	Overview		67
16.2.	Checklist of Dos and Don'ts		69

17.	**Prohibition of Discrimination in the Workplace**	69
	17.1. Overview of Anti-discrimination Laws	69
	17.2. Age Discrimination	71
	17.3. Race Discrimination	71
	17.4. Sex Discrimination/Sexual Harassment	72
	17.5. Handicap and Disability Discrimination	72
	17.6. National Extraction or Social Origin Discrimination	73
	17.7. Religious Discrimination	73
	17.8. Military Status Discrimination	74
	17.9. Pregnancy Discrimination	74
	17.10. Marital Status Discrimination	75
	17.11. Sexual Orientation Discrimination	75
	17.12. Retaliation/Victimization	75
	17.13. Fair Work Legislation	76
	17.14. Bullying and Harassment	76
	17.15. Sexual Harassment	77
	17.16. Constructive Discharge/Constructive Dismissal	79
	17.17. Checklist of Dos and Don'ts	79
18.	**Smoking in the Workplace**	80
	18.1. Overview	80
	18.2. Checklist of Dos and Don'ts	82
19.	**Use of Drugs and Alcohol in the Workplace**	83
	19.1. Overview: Use of Drugs and Alcohol in the Workplace	83
	19.2. Checklist of Dos and Don'ts	85
20.	**AIDS, HIV, SARS, Blood-Borne Pathogens**	85
	20.1. Overview	85
	20.2. Checklist of Dos and Don'ts	88
21.	**Dress and Grooming Requirements**	89
	21.1. Overview	89
	21.2. Checklist of Dos and Don'ts	90
22.	**Privacy, Technology and Transfer of Personal Data**	90
	22.1. Privacy Rights of Employees	90
	22.2. Checklist of Dos and Don'ts	95
23.	**Workplace Investigations for Complaints of Discrimination, Harassment, Fraud, Theft and Whistle-Blowing**	95
	23.1. Overview	95
	23.2. Checklist of Dos and Don'ts	96

24. Affirmative Action Non-discrimination Requirements 96
24.1. Overview 96
24.2. Checklist of Dos and Don'ts 97

25. Resolution of Labour, Discrimination and Employment Disputes: Litigation, Arbitration, Mediation and Conciliation 98
25.1. Internal Dispute Resolution Processes 98
25.2. Mediation and Conciliation 99
25.3. Arbitration 100
25.4. Litigation 100
25.5. Fines, Penalties and Damages 101
25.6. Checklist of Dos and Don'ts 102

26. Employer Record-Keeping, Data Protection and Employee Access to Personnel Files and Records 102
26.1. Overview 102
26.2. Personnel Files 103
26.3. Confidentiality Rules 103
26.4. Employee Access 103

27. Required Notices and Postings 104
27.1. Overview 104
27.2. Checklist of Dos and Don'ts 105

Australia

AUTHORS

John Tuck

John is the National Practice Group Leader of the Corrs Employment & Labour team. John is a recognized leader in the field of employment & labour. He brings practical and strategic thinking to complex enquiries, integrity issues, crisis management, workplace issues and litigation.

Whether it is advising on complex investigations, national employment strategies, developing industrial plans for multibillion dollar infrastructure projects or Royal Commissions and Inquiries, John possesses a unique perspective that can come only with extensive experience.

This is just one of the reasons why John has been trusted by State and Federal Governments and major Australian employers, including Boeing, Australia Post, Downer EDI, Multiplex, NAB, University of Melbourne, and Exxon Mobil.

ADDRESS

Corrs Chambers Westgarth
567 Collins Street
Melbourne VIC 3000
Australia
Tel.: +61 3 9672 3257
E-mail: john.tuck@corrs.com.au
Web: www.corrs.com.au

Stephen Price

Stephen Price has over twenty-five years' experience as a workplace relations lawyer and is focused on providing practical and commercially focussed employment and industrial relations advice. Stephen has particular experience as an employment law litigator and has conducted some of Australia's leading employment and industrial cases. He has wide experience providing advice on business acquisitions, mergers, internal investigations and occupational health and safety to a range of leading Australian and overseas companies on all aspects of industrial and employment law.

ADDRESS

Corrs Chambers Westgarth
Quay Quarter Tower
Level 37/50 Bridge Street
Sydney NSW 2000
Australia
Tel.: +61 2 9210 6236
E-mail: stephen.price@corrs.com.au
Web: www.corrs.com.au

Jack de Flamingh

Jack de Flamingh graduated from the University of New South Wales in Commerce (Finance)/Laws in 1996. Jack is a Workplace Relations Partner at Corrs Chambers Westgarth, where he specializes in industrial relations and occupational health and safety law. Jack advises clients in a range of critical industries and is a regular speaker at industry seminars on safety and employment law topics, more recently focusing on changes made to Australian industrial relations laws.

ADDRESS

Corrs Chambers Westgarth
Quay Quarter Tower
Level 37/50 Bridge Street
Sydney NSW 2000
Australia
Tel.: +61 2 9210 6192
E-mail: Jack.de.Flamingh@corrs.com.au
Web: www.corrs.com.au
Tel.: +61 402 029 362
E-mail: rosemary.roach@corrs.com.au
Web: www.corrs.com.au

Nick Le Mare

Nick has extensive experience in industries that are at the forefront of workplace relations – mining, construction, aviation, transport and logistics.

In addition to his law firm experience, Nick has significant experience in-house. He was General Manager Workplace Relations for Virgin Australia during a time of enormous upheaval in that industry. He has also been General Counsel and a member of the Executive Leadership Team at Queensland Rail. Nick is an experienced workplace relations lawyer with a proven ability to deliver results.

ADDRESS

Corrs Chambers Westgarth
One One Eagle Street
Brisbane, QLD
Australia
Tel.: +61 7 3229 9786
E-mail: nick.lemare@corrs.com.au
Web: www.corrs.com.au

Legal Compliance in Australia

1. LEGAL FRAMEWORK: EMPLOYMENT LAWS*

In Australia, the regulation of labour, or 'workplace relations', is shared between the federal legislature and the states. As a result, there are both federal and state statutes that regulate most employers. However, following significant reforms between 2006 and 2009, practically all companies are now governed by the federal *Fair Work Act 2009* (Cth) (FW Act) in respect of laws regulating engagement, dismissals, minimum terms and conditions and collective bargaining. Employers covered by the FW Act are known as 'National System Employers'. As a general rule, all employers are now National System Employers, except for some state public sector employers and unincorporated employers.

State laws continue to regulate workplace health and safety and discrimination in employment (with discrimination also being regulated by federal laws).

The Australian legal system is a common law system, and the fundamental rules with respect to the making and terminating of employment contracts are established by the common law.

In addition, however, the FW Act:

- contains 11 'National Employment Standards' (NES) which prescribe the minimum leave, public holidays, notice of termination, redundancy pay and maximum weekly hours for all employees;
- allows for the making of 'modern awards' which provide for more detailed regulation of certain industries and occupations;
- allows an employer and its employees to make enterprise agreements that may override applicable modern awards (but not the NES);
- provides for rules regulating trade unions and collective bargaining;

* This chapter does not include temporary changes introduced to respond to COVID-19.

– provides an 'unfair dismissal' jurisdiction for employees who earn below a statutory threshold or are covered by an enterprise agreement or modern award.

For publicly listed companies, further regulations on pay and employment conditions for senior executive employees are contained in the *Corporations Act 2001* (Cth) and Australian Stock Exchange Listing Rules.

The various modern awards made under the FW Act apply to most categories of employees, other than management and some professional staff. They typically regulate hours of work, shift and overtime penalties and minimum wages and allowances. Modern awards are made and kept updated by the Fair Work Commission (FWC).

The employer can make an enterprise agreement with its employees that excludes (or supplements) the terms of the otherwise applicable modern award. Employees and employers may appoint a bargaining representative to assist them in these negotiations. These agreements then need to be approved by a majority of the employees at the enterprise and then are assessed using a 'better off overall' test against the applicable modern award prior to becoming operational. Enterprise agreements have a maximum duration of four years. Their expiration date is, however, 'nominal', in that the agreements continue after this period until actively terminated or replaced.

Employers must make contributions to an employee's retirement benefits fund under the *Superannuation Guarantee (Administration) Act 1992 (Cth)* and the *Superannuation Guarantee Charge Act 1992 (Cth).*

Under state laws, employers are required to take out mandatory workers' compensation insurance for all employees. Depending on the size of the employer's workforce and the particular state, employers may also be liable for a state 'payroll tax'.

2. CONTRACTS OF EMPLOYMENT

2.1. Overview

In Australia, the employee and employer relationship will be formed where the parties enter into a contract of service, or employment contract, which may be written, oral or a combination of both. There are a number of different types of employment, including full-time, part-time and casual. The FW Act has recently been amended to include a definition of casual employee (*see* section 15A). Pursuant to that section, a person will be a casual employee if there is 'no firm advance commitment to continuing and indefinite work according to an agreed pattern of work for the person' and an offer to work on this basis is accepted by the employee. The employment contract may be ongoing, for a fixed or maximum period, or for the performance of a specific task.

Employment contracts include express terms and implied terms. The express terms of the contract generally describe the employee's position, commencement date, remuneration, hours of work, leave entitlements and termination conditions.

There are terms implied by law in all employment contracts, to the extent that they are not excluded by express or implied agreement, industrial instrument (such as awards and enterprise agreements) or law. These terms are often expressed as duties owed by the employer (e.g., duty of care) and employee (e.g., duty to obey a reasonable direction). Terms may also be implied in the employment contract from the facts and circumstances of a particular case.

Generally, an employer cannot unilaterally vary the contractual employment terms. However, the parties may at any time vary the terms of the employment contract by agreement. Further, some flexibility is provided because the employer has the power to give lawful and reasonable directions to an employee, for example, as to how work is to be performed.

The terms of the employment contract must always be read subject to the requirements of applicable workplace relations laws and industrial instruments. These laws and industrial instruments set minimum standards that will prevail over the terms of the employment contract. The parties cannot agree to contract out of the minimum entitlements prescribed by a law or industrial instrument.

2.2. Written and Oral Employment Contracts

A valid employment contract can be entirely oral; there is no requirement for a written contract at all. However, in some cases, an industrial instrument may require notification by the employer or an agreement in writing between the parties about particular terms.

The terms of an employment contract in a particular case may be partly written, partly oral and partly determined by statute and/or an industrial instrument. A written contract does not necessarily preclude earlier terms orally agreed between the parties.

For a majority of Australian workers, their terms and conditions are prescribed by an industrial instrument – an award or agreement. Thus, employees in many cases will not have a comprehensive written employment contract. The terms of industrial instruments are not incorporated into and are not enforceable as terms of the employment contract unless expressly agreed between the parties.

Employees who are not covered by an industrial instrument, typically professional and managerial workers, will usually have a written employment contract setting out the key terms of their engagement.

2.3. EMPLOYEE HANDBOOKS

Many employers in Australia have employee handbooks or human resource manuals, comprising policies and procedures which may address a broad range of matters such as:

- employee entitlements – for example, leave, remuneration, travel and expenses;
- employee behaviour – for example, workplace health and safety, equal opportunity and codes of conduct;
- employee management – for example, recruitment and selection, performance and disciplinary processes.

An employer may implement and require employees to comply with policies and procedures as lawful and reasonable directions; otherwise, a party may seek to enforce the terms of a policy or procedure on the basis that it is expressly or impliedly incorporated into the terms and conditions of the employment contract. This may occur, for example, when an employee is seeking to enforce an entitlement provided by a policy, such as redundancy pay. Whether the terms of a policy are enforceable in the contract will depend on the circumstances of the case, including the terms of the policy and the employment contract.

Employers in Australia will often include an express term in their employment contracts that their policies and procedures are not incorporated as terms of the contract and may be varied unilaterally by the employer from time to time.

2.4. JOB DESCRIPTIONS

Many employers in Australia have job or position descriptions that set out the duties and responsibilities of employees. These are generally drafted in broad terms and are often included as an attachment or appendix to an employee's employment contract.

In addition, industrial instruments usually include a job description or 'classification' for each employee covered by the instrument and prescribe wage rates according to the employee's classification. An industrial instrument may prescribe a number of different levels of remuneration within each classification.

An employer may be required by the terms of an industrial instrument to notify the employee of their classification under the instrument.

2.5. Offer Letters

There is generally no requirement in Australia that an employer must provide a prospective employee with a written offer letter. However, in many cases, an employer will do so, and the terms of the offer, once accepted by the employee, will form the express terms of the employment contract.

An offer of employment may be made subject to conditions, for example, that an employee passes a medical examination. The employer must ensure that such requirements do not violate other laws, such as anti-discrimination laws.

An employer may withdraw an offer of employment before it is accepted by the prospective employee. However, in some instances, an employer could be estopped from denying the existence of a contract of employment or may be found to have misled or deceived the prospective employee about the employment, and the employer may be liable for damages.

2.6. Checklist of Dos and Don'ts

- It is advisable to record key terms and conditions of employment in writing, particularly for senior and managerial employees who are not covered by any industrial instrument.
- Employers must be familiar with the minimum standards prescribed by workplace relations laws and industrial instruments. These will prevail over the terms of the employment contract.
- Employee handbooks should be drafted with care, and consideration should be given as to whether the terms of policies and procedures are intended by the employer to be incorporated as terms of the employment contract.

3. RECRUITING, INTERVIEWING, SCREENING AND HIRING EMPLOYEES

3.1. Overview

While there is no specific statutory regulation of the recruitment, screening or hiring process in Australia, employers should be mindful that job applicants may make a claim against the employer if an applicant considers that they have been discriminated against.

3.2. Recruiting

Employers are able to advertise new or vacant positions using a range of resources such as newspaper or internet advertisements, intranet sites, employee referrals, use of recruitment agencies, use of executive search firms or general 'word of mouth'. From time to time, industrial instruments or policies may provide that new or vacant positions must be advertised internally before the positions are advertised externally.

3.3. Employment Applications

Generally, Australian employers will ask applicants to complete an application form and/or submit a resume or curriculum vitae.

The content of application forms will vary depending on the nature of the position and the employer's business. Generally, an application form will request that the employee provide details of the applicant's qualifications and experience. Employers should be careful to ensure that the application form does not contain any questions or requests for information that would indicate that applicants with certain characteristics (such as those with carer's responsibilities, persons of a particular race or with other protected attributes) would not be selected for the role. This could form the basis for a claim of discrimination.

Typically, job applicants will also have access to a position description at the time that the application is made, which sets out the duties and responsibilities of the position and the qualifications, experience and attributes required to perform the role.

The application form should also include a statement which deals with how the information collected in the application will be dealt with in accordance with Australian privacy laws or should refer the applicant to the employer's privacy policy (*see* section 22).

3.4. Pre-employment Enquiries

In Australia, state and federal discrimination laws make it unlawful for employers to refuse to employ persons on the basis of certain personal characteristics (such as age, sex, marital status, family responsibilities or pregnancy) unless an exemption applies. In certain states, it is unlawful to seek information which could be used to discriminate against a person.

For this reason, an employer should avoid making enquiries during an interview in relation to personal characteristics (such as the applicant's age, sex or marital status). Interview questions should be limited to ascertaining whether the person has the relevant qualifications, experience and non-discriminatory attributes to perform the position.

As to the list of personal characteristics which could ground a discrimination claim in Australia, *see* section 17.

An employer should also be mindful that records created during the recruitment process may be subject to Australian privacy legislation, *see* section 22.

3.5. Pre-employment Tests and Examinations

In Australia, an employer may request applicants to undergo pre-employment tests and exams to determine whether an applicant has the proper skills and abilities to perform a particular job. This may include psychometric testing.

In addition, an employer may request a pre-employment medical examination and drug/alcohol testing prior to an offer of employment being made. Drug and alcohol addiction can be ground for a claim of discrimination in Australia. Therefore, rejecting an applicant on the basis of a drug/alcohol test should be linked to the inherent requirements of the role. Employers should ensure that applicants are not excluded on the basis of any physical or mental disability, unless the disability would prohibit the applicant from performing the inherent requirements of the position, without reasonable accommodation.

3.6. Background, Reference and Credit Checks

In Australia, it is both permissible and common for an employer to ask about an applicant's previous experience, request documents confirming previous employment, request personal references, undertake credit check references, and with certain limitations, undertake a criminal background check. While refusing to make an offer of employment on the basis of a criminal background check is not necessarily unlawful, it could expose an employer to an enquiry being made by the Australian Human Rights Commission or another like body if the criminal background is not relevant to the applicant's capacity to perform the position. Relevantly, in some Australian jurisdictions, it is unlawful to discriminate against a prospective employee on the basis of a 'spent' conviction. A conviction will be spent if it no longer appears on an individual's criminal record.

3.7. Interviewing

It is common for Australian employers to conduct face-to-face or telephone interviews with applicants who, based on the information set out in the application form, appear suitable for the role. Often, more than one interview will be conducted. While an employer is free to conduct the interview in any manner, it is important that those conducting the interview have received adequate training to ensure that no questions are asked that could ground a discrimination claim. All questions asked during an interview should be limited to ascertaining whether the applicant has the skills, experience and non-discriminatory attributes to perform the position.

Further, those conducting the interview on behalf of the employer should be careful to ensure that they do not make any statements that could mislead the applicant about the availability, nature, terms or conditions of, or any other matter relating to, the employment.

3.8. Hiring Procedures

Employers should always inform employees that they are being hired subject to the terms of a contract of employment and any relevant industrial instruments that may apply to the employee. Further, if the offer of employment is subject to the satisfaction of other criteria (e.g., reference checks or a drug and alcohol test), this should be made clear to the applicant at the time that the offer of employment is made. The new employee must be provided with a copy of the Fair Work Information Statement and will also need to complete a tax declaration form.

3.9. Fines and Penalties

Applicants who believe they were not successful with their application due to a discriminatory reason may file a discrimination claim in state or federal tribunals, which may result in court proceedings. Depending on the nature of the allegation, an applicant may also commence proceedings for a contravention of the 'general protection' provisions of federal legislation (as to the general protections, *see* section 25 of this Chapter).

Applicants may seek damages for any actual loss suffered as a consequence of the employer's failure to hire the applicant, general damages (for injury, humiliation, etc.) and, in certain circumstances, exemplary damages. Depending on the jurisdiction, the applicant may also be able to recover legal costs. A court or tribunal may also order that an apology be given or order that discriminatory conduct or practices cease.

3.10. Checklist of Dos and Don'ts

- Ensure that employment applications do not require the provision of any information which could be used to ground a discrimination claim.
- Before an interview, employers should ensure that any questions only relate to ascertaining whether the applicant has the qualifications, experience and non-discriminatory attributes to perform the position.
- Those conducting interviews should be provided with training to ensure that discriminatory questions are not inadvertently asked of an applicant.
- Employers should ensure that any background checks and pre-employment testing are relevant to ascertaining whether the applicant is able to perform the position.
- Misleading representations as to the availability, nature, terms or conditions of or any other matter relating to the employment must not be made.
- It is preferable, but not essential that at least two people conduct the interview on behalf of the employer so that one representative is able to take notes of the questions asked and the applicant's response.

4. MANAGING PERFORMANCE/CONDUCT

4.1. Overview

Effective performance management has a number of benefits, such as:

- opening lines of communication between employees and managers to discuss progress and/or grievances and provide feedback;
- linking an employee's personal goals to the organization's broader business objectives with the aim of bringing about a more effective workplace and increased employee satisfaction;
- identifying 'high potential' employees who may be suitable for future manager/supervisory positions;
- obtaining feedback to improve areas of business/work practices;
- reducing the likelihood of successful legal challenges to termination, for example, discrimination claims and claims of unfair dismissal or for contravention of the 'general protections' provisions.

4.2. Coaching and Counselling

When an employee is not meeting the required level of performance, or an employee's conduct is unsatisfactory, it is appropriate in the first instance to manage employee performance unless the performance or conduct issues are sufficiently serious to warrant a warning.

Performance counselling is most effective when a manager/supervisor acts immediately to address an issue of unsatisfactory performance or conduct.

Details of any performance management should be recorded, a copy of that record supplied to the employee and a copy retained in a personnel file.

4.3. Written Evaluations

An important step in the performance management process is written evaluations that bring together issues that have arisen and formalize standards and objectives moving forward. Typically, a written evaluation will be in the form of an annual performance review.

Written evaluations on an annual basis manage performance and inform the employee as to his/her status within an organization. They also help to identify an employee's strengths and weaknesses, training needs and career aspirations.

When preparing performance evaluations, employers should use a process that is based on job-related criteria, rather than individual employee characteristics. If this is done, properly documented and completed honestly, performance evaluations should help prevent discrimination claims or claims of unfair dismissal or for contravention of the 'general protections' provisions (should this eventuate). If an evaluation does not adequately inform the employee of their status, it can have negative consequences in any potential litigation. However, an annual written evaluation should not be a substitute for ongoing counselling during the course of a year.

4.4. Warnings and Suspensions

Where an employee's performance or conduct is below what is acceptable to the employer, and there has not been a positive response after counselling, a warning should be issued to the employee.

Often it may be appropriate to provide a verbal warning as part of the counselling process. However, written warnings will usually be appropriate where:

- counselling or a verbal warning has not achieved the required level of performance;
- the level of performance is so poor, or conduct unacceptable, that it justifies a written warning.

A warning letter should contain the following information:

- refer to any previous counselling or verbal warnings;
- clearly identify itself as a letter of warning;
- clearly identify that any future incidents of unsatisfactory performance or conduct may lead to further disciplinary action;
- outline and provide specific details of the unsatisfactory performance or conduct issue;
- outline and provide details about the standards required of the organization.

A final written warning will be appropriate where, despite earlier warnings, an employee's performance or general conduct has not improved or the particular instance of unsatisfactory performance or conduct warrants a final warning.

A final written warning should contain the following information:

- refer to any counselling or prior warnings;
- detail the employee's unsatisfactory performance or conduct;
- if appropriate, detail the required improvements and the time frame within which the improvements are required;
- identify that it is a final written warning and any further occasions of unsatisfactory performance may lead to termination of employment.

Generally speaking, it will not be appropriate to suspend an employee who is engaged in performance counselling (as opposed to investigating serious conduct issues). There is no common law right to suspend an employee without pay as a disciplinary measure. Suspension may be appropriate in circumstances where an employer is investigating allegations of serious misconduct. In those circumstances, the employee should be suspended with full pay.

There are circumstances where an employer may lawfully 'stand down' an employee. 'Stand down' means to not require the employee to attend work and stop payment to him or her, without terminating the employee's employment. There is no common law right to 'stand down' an employee. A 'stand down' can only be imposed in accordance with the terms of applicable legislation (*see* section 524, FW Act), an enterprise agreement or a contract of employment. The capacity to stand down an employee may be enlivened where an employee cannot be usefully employed because of industrial action, a breakdown of machinery or equipment for which an employer cannot reasonably be held responsible and a stoppage of work for which the employer cannot reasonably be held responsible. It does not extend to disciplinary or performance matters.

4.5. Checklist of Dos and Don'ts

- Act immediately to address issues of performance or conduct.
- Afford procedural fairness to an employee. This means clearly identifying what the problem is and what is expected by the employer.
- Attempt to agree on performance targets and take steps to ensure the issue does not occur again.
- For performance matters, set a review date to monitor performance.
- If unsatisfactory performance or conduct does not improve, issue a written warning. In that warning, refer to any previous counselling, the issue and what is required and make it clear that unless the employee's performance improves to meet the required standard, termination of employment is possible.
- Performance evaluations and warnings should be honest and accurate and provide the employee with sufficient information so that the employee understands what is required of him or her in the role.

5. TERMINATION OF EMPLOYEES FOR PERFORMANCE OR DISCIPLINARY REASONS

5.1. Overview

Where an employee breaches an obligation due to misconduct or failure to perform work to a satisfactory standard, employers may impose disciplinary sanctions that, in extreme circumstances, can extend to termination of the employment contract. Australia has ratified the International Labour Organization's Termination of Employment Convention 1982 (No. 158), and thereby adopted the principle that 'an employee's employment shall not be terminated unless there is a valid reason for such termination connected with the capacity or conduct of the worker or based on the operational requirements of the undertaking, establishment or service'.

The FW Act provides remedies that require employers to act fairly in terminating employment and which otherwise prohibit terminations for particular reasons (discriminatory or other unlawful reasons). Each state in Australia also has discrimination legislation that prohibits termination for discriminatory reasons such as sex, race, disability and age.

5.2. Separation/Severance Pay

The principal statutory remedies are claims alleging unfair dismissal or for contravention of the 'general protections' provisions. 'Unfair dismissal' is a claim made that the termination of employment was 'harsh, unjust or unreasonable'. 'General protections' claims include claims for adverse action (which includes termination of employment) for a prohibited ground. Prohibited grounds include discrimination against the employee on the basis of age, race, sexual preference, religion, trade union membership, lawful industrial activity, temporary absence from work due to illness or for the exercise of a 'workplace right' (*see* section 11.6).

Notice

In most cases, an employee's employment may be terminated by giving the proper period of notice, unless the conduct is serious misconduct in which case, the employment may be terminated immediately without notice.

A minimum statutory notice period is prescribed in the FW Act. The required period of notice is between one and four weeks, depending on the employee's length of service with the employer. The period of notice is increased by one week if the employee is over 45 years old and has completed at least two years of continuous service. In practice, employers often pay the amount an employee would have received during the notice period in lieu of notice in order to bring the contract to an end immediately. Notice of termination is not required for serious misconduct.

Some employees may have a longer notice period set out in their contract of employment (particularly senior employees) or an industrial award or agreement which applies to their employment. In those circumstances, the employer must provide the notice period specified in the contract or industrial instrument.

Statutory Entitlements

Upon termination of employment, employees will be entitled to be paid out of their accrued statutory entitlements, which will include annual leave and long service leave (*see* section 11). The employee's contract of employment or applicable industrial instrument may provide a more favourable leave entitlement, which must be paid upon termination.

Other Severance Payments

An additional payment may be due where an employee is terminated by reason of redundancy (*see* section 6).

5.3. Fines and Penalties

Termination of employment will rarely be a basis for the imposition of fines and penalties. The FW Act contains civil penalty provisions which may apply where a termination is motivated by a prohibited reason.

Civil penalties may also be imposed where termination of employment is otherwise in breach of an industrial instrument. For example, an enterprise agreement may specify a particular process for the termination of employment, including steps such as consulting with union representatives.

In the case of unfair dismissal, FWC may order compensation of up to six months' salary up to a total of (presently) AUD $83,750 or reinstatement and back pay.

Unfair Dismissal

The FW Act sets out who is covered by unfair dismissal laws, the elements that constitute unfair dismissal and the procedure for making a claim with FWC.

An employee who qualifies to bring a claim for unfair dismissal under the FW Act (i.e., meets all the eligibility criteria) must establish that their dismissal was 'harsh, unjust or unreasonable' in order to be entitled to a remedy. To be eligible to bring an unfair dismissal claim, an employee must have been employed for over six months (twelve months in the case of a small business employer, which is an employer with less than fifteen employees) and either be covered by an award or other industrial instrument or earn less than the 'high-income threshold' (presently AUD $167,500 but increases each year broadly in line with inflation).

An unfair dismissal claim is lodged with FWC. The factors that FWC will consider in determining whether a dismissal was 'harsh, unjust or unreasonable' are as follows:

- whether there was a 'valid reason' for the dismissal related to the person's capacity or conduct (including the effect of this conduct on the safety and welfare of other employees);
- whether the person was notified of that reason;
- whether the person was given an opportunity to respond to any reason related to the capacity or conduct of the person;
- any unreasonable refusal by the employer to allow the person to have a support person present to assist in any discussions relating to dismissal;
- if the dismissal was related to unsatisfactory performance by the person – whether the person had been warned about that unsatisfactory performance before the dismissal;
- the degree to which the size of the employer's enterprise would be likely to impact the procedures followed in effecting the dismissal;
- the degree to which the absence of dedicated human resource management specialists or expertise in the enterprise would be likely to impact the procedures followed in effecting the dismissal; and
- any other matters that FWC considers relevant.

An employee cannot bring an unfair dismissal claim if the termination is a 'genuine redundancy'. As to the circumstances giving rise to a 'genuine redundancy' within the meaning of the FW Act, *see* section 6.

General Protections

Whereas the provisions dealing with 'unfair dismissal' under the FW Act only apply to certain eligible employees, the provisions relating to 'general protections' apply to all employees and employers in Australia. It is important for dismissals to be made for genuine misconduct and poor performance reasons, rather than for any reasons that may be construed as discriminatory.

The FW Act provides that claims for contravention of the 'general protections' provisions can be made where a person has been dismissed on the basis of a prohibited reason (*see* section 11.6).

There is a reverse onus of proof for these provisions meaning that, if it is alleged that a termination was made for a prohibited reason, it will be presumed to have been taken for that reason, unless the employer proves otherwise.

There is no limitation on the amount of compensation that can be awarded if it is found that there was a contravention of the 'general protections' provisions.

5.4. Checklist of Dos and Don'ts

- To terminate an employee's employment, the employer must consider both substantive reasons and procedural fairness.
- Ensure that you are aware of any contractual or industrial instrument provisions relating to termination and that the statutory or contractual notice requirements are met.
- Provide warnings prior to dismissing an employee for unsatisfactory performance or conduct.
- Do not include discriminatory reasons or any other prohibited reason in your decision-making processes. Be aware of the reverse onus which may apply to an unlawful termination claim and ensure that your decision-making process can withstand scrutiny.
- A methodical and detailed investigation shows that the matter has been thoroughly considered, and the decision to terminate is not taken lightly or partially.
- In situations of poor employee performance, organizations need to document and substantiate the actions taken.

- Ask whether company work rules and policies are known by all employees. Have other employees been disciplined or terminated for the same reason?
- Consider whether the employee made any complaint which could provide the basis for an unfair dismissal or 'general protections' claim.

6. LAYOFFS, REDUCTIONS IN FORCE AND/OR REDUNDANCIES AS A RESULT OF JOB ELIMINATIONS OR OTHER RESTRUCTURING

6.1. Overview

As outlined in section 5 above, many Australian employees are protected from harsh or arbitrary dismissal under the unfair dismissal provisions in the FW Act. However, these provisions do not restrict an employer's ability to lawfully terminate an employee's employment on the ground of 'genuine redundancy'. Before terminating for genuine redundancy, employers must comply with the information and consultation obligations under modern awards, enterprise agreements and the FW Act.

Employees terminated for genuine redundancy also have statutory rights to minimum periods of notice prior to termination of employment (*see* section 5) and severance pay (*see* below).

6.2. Reductions in Force/Layoffs/Job Eliminations

6.2.1. Genuine Redundancy Exclusion from Unfair Dismissal Claims

(*See* section 389, FW Act)

Genuine redundancies are excluded from the unfair dismissal regime. To qualify as a 'genuine redundancy', the following circumstances must apply:

- the employer no longer requires the employee's job to be performed by anyone because of changes in the operational requirements of the employer's business;
- the employer has complied with any obligation in an applicable modern award or enterprise agreement to consult about the redundancy (*see* further section 6.2(b) below); and
- the employee could not reasonably have been redeployed within the business of the employer or an associated entity of the employer.

Employers can terminate employees for redundancy as a result of a downturn in work, a downturn in sales or profits, the completion of a project, a site or business closure, outsourcing and other forms of restructuring. Essentially, an employee's position will be redundant when the employer no longer wishes for the employee's role (as it is currently constituted) to be performed by anyone. However, certain procedural requirements must be met in order to rely on the genuine redundancy exclusion from federal unfair dismissal claims.

Employees who are to be made redundant have to be selected according to fair and objective criteria; for example, an employer cannot select employees for redundancy based on union membership or age.

6.2.2. Information and Consultation Requirements about Major Workplace Changes in Modern Awards and Enterprise Agreements

Employers covered by modern awards and enterprise agreements are subject to requirements to provide information to, and consult with, employees and their representatives (including trade unions) before implementing any proposals to introduce 'major workplace changes' in production, programme, organization, structure or technology that are likely to have significant effects on employees. This standard information/consultation clause has been inserted in all modern awards.

Parties to enterprise agreements may choose to adopt the model consultation term (set out in the *Fair Work Regulations 2009* (Cth)), or negotiate their own provision in an enterprise agreement which meets the requirements of the FW Act (*see* section 205(1), FW Act).

Modern awards and enterprise agreements create obligations to inform and consult – not to gain the consent of employees or their representatives to managerial decisions. However, where employers fail to observe the information/consultation requirements in an award or enterprise agreement, employees and/or unions may be able to obtain an injunction preventing the implementation of proposed redundancies and other workplace changes until proper consultation occurs (*see* section 6.3 below).

6.2.3. FW Act Information and Consultation Requirements

Under the FW Act, employers have further information and consultation obligations in relation to large-scale redundancies. An employer must notify the federal government agency responsible for providing unemployment assistance (Centrelink) where the employer has decided to terminate the employment of fifteen or more employees for economic, technological, structural or similar reasons (*see* section 27).

FWC may make orders regarding meeting consultation obligations where an employer has decided to make fifteen or more employees redundant and the employer has failed to meet its obligation to:

- inform any union of which the employees are a member of the proposed terminations, the reasons for them, the number of categories of employees affected and their timing; and
- consult with the union(s) in relation to measures to avert or minimize the proposed terminations and measures to mitigate their adverse effects.

Both information provision and consultation must occur as soon as practicable after the employer makes such a decision, and before terminating any of the employees. If the employer does not comply with those obligations, FWC may make any orders that it considers appropriate to put the employees and the union(s) in the same position as if there had been compliance with these information or consultation obligations. However, FWC may not make orders reinstating any of the employees, or requiring the withdrawal of termination notices, payment in lieu of reinstatement or severance pay, or the disclosure of confidential information (including commercially sensitive information or personal information) by an employer.

6.2.4. Severance Pay

Employees covered by the FW Act have the right to be paid a minimum severance payment when their employment is terminated because the employer no longer requires the employee's job to be done by anyone; or because the employer has become insolvent or bankrupt. The amount of severance pay is based on an employee's period of continuous service with their employer, according to the following scale:

Employee's Period of Continuous Service with the Employer on Termination	*Redundancy Pay*
At least 1 year but less than 2 years	4 weeks
At least 2 years but less than 3 years	6 weeks
At least 3 years but less than 4 years	7 weeks
At least 4 years but less than 5 years	8 weeks
At least 5 years but less than 6 years	10 weeks
At least 6 years but less than 7 years	11 weeks
At least 7 years but less than 8 years	13 weeks

Employee's Period of Continuous Service with the Employer on Termination	*Redundancy Pay*
At least 8 years but less than 9 years	14 weeks
At least 9 years but less than 10 years	16 weeks
At least 10 years	12 weeks[1]

However, these statutory redundancy pay entitlements do not apply to certain types of employees, including casual employees, fixed-term employees, and those working in small businesses (i.e., less than fifteen employees). Further, the statutory redundancy pay entitlements operate as minimum standards only, and employers covered by enterprise agreements are commonly required to provide employees with more favourable redundancy pay entitlements.

6.3. Fines and Penalties

The following constitute breaches of relevant 'civil remedy' provisions of the FW Act:

- failure by an employer to observe the information consultation requirements applicable to proposed workplace changes in a modern award or an enterprise agreement;
- an employer's termination of the employment of fifteen or more employees without notifying Centrelink;
- failure by an employer to provide employees with their minimum statutory entitlement to severance pay.

Under the FW Act, specified parties (including a Fair Work Inspector appointed by the Fair Work Ombudsman (FWO), employees affected by a contravention of a civil remedy provision and unions) can bring proceedings in the Federal Court or Federal Circuit Court if there is a breach of the civil remedy provisions. Such proceedings may result in the imposition of civil penalties of up to (presently) AUD 82,500 for corporations and (presently) AUD 16,500 for individuals.

By reason of the *Fair Work Amendment (Protecting Vulnerable Workers) Act 2017* (Cth), penalties for a 'serious contravention' of the FW Act can result in a penalty of (presently) AUD 165,000 (for individuals) and (presently) AUD 825,000 (for a corporation). A 'serious contravention' happens when:

1. The amount of redundancy pay reduces after ten years' service as this is the point at which employees generally become entitled to a period of long service leave (or payments in lieu of long service leave upon termination). As to long service leave, *see* s. 11.

- the person or business knew they were contravening an obligation under workplace law;
- the contravention was part of a systematic pattern of conduct affecting one or more people.

Serious contraventions may include breaches of:

- the NES;
- a modern award;
- an enterprise agreement;
- a workplace determination;
- a national minimum wage order;
- an equal remuneration wage order;
- method and frequency of paying wages;
- the section that says an employer must not require employees to spend any of their money or pay back their wages if it is unreasonable ('cashback schemes');
- guarantees of annual earnings;
- record-keeping requirements; and
- payslip requirements.

In addition, the courts may make orders (in appropriate cases and depending on the particular FW Act provisions involved) for the payment of compensation or the reinstatement of employees; or the courts can issue injunctions to prevent a breach of a civil remedy provision from occurring.

The power of the courts to order injunctions could be significant in the context of non-compliance with information and consultation obligations, as they may enable employees/unions to prevent the implementation of management restructuring decisions until these obligations are followed.

6.4. Checklist of Dos and Don'ts

- To avoid unfair dismissal claims, employers should ensure that any workforce size reductions/layoffs meet the requirements for genuine redundancies under the FW Act. This means ensuring that consultation obligations are complied with and there are no reasonable redeployment options.
- Check the terms of applicable modern awards and enterprise agreements, and ensure that when implementing any decisions relating to major workplace changes, any award or agreement information and consultation requirements are complied with.
- When making fifteen or more employees redundant, notify Centrelink and inform/consult with relevant unions to avoid the imposition of FWC orders.

– Account in advance for the payment of minimum statutory entitlements to severance pay to employees in the event of redundancy.

7. LABOUR AND EMPLOYMENT LAW RAMIFICATIONS UPON ACQUISITION OR SALE OF A BUSINESS

7.1. Overview

The sale of a business will generally take place by way of a share sale or asset sale. In a share sale, the identity of the employing entity does not change. Employees' contracts and industrial instruments continue – subject only to any change of control provisions that may exist in the employment contracts of senior executives.

In an asset sale, however, employees will need to cease being employed by the seller and commence employment with the purchaser. This requires their agreement. Further, there can be a number of ramifications including:

(1) the purchaser becoming bound by the industrial instruments that bound the old employer in respect of the transferring employees;
(2) the leave entitlements of employees being transferred to the purchaser or paid out to the employees by the seller;
(3) in certain circumstances, the seller being obliged to make redundancy payments to its employees.

7.2. Acquisition of a Business

When acquiring a business in an asset sale, a purchaser will need to procure the employment of the employees of the seller by making them an offer of employment. It will then need to consider the following issues:

The Transfer of Industrial Instruments

Australian law provides for the transfer of most industrial instruments where there is a 'transfer of business' between two employers.

Generally speaking, there will be a transfer of business, if employees of the seller become employees of the buyer within three months of their employment with the seller ending, and one of the following circumstances exists:

(a) there is a transfer of assets (or the beneficial use of assets) between the old employer and the new employer and the assets relate to, or are used in connection with, work performed by transferring employees;
(b) the employees are transferred as part of an 'outsourcing' or 'in-sourcing' endeavour; or

(c) the new employer is an 'associated entity' of the old employer (i.e., a company in the same corporate group or a company that has an investment in and significant influence over another company).

When there is a transfer of business, an industrial instrument (the 'transferable instrument') that applies to a transferring employee will transfer to the new employer and will continue to cover that employee in the performance of the transferring work.

The transferable instrument may also cover new employees of the new employer, who are not transferring employees if:

- the new employee will perform work the same as the work done by transferring employees; and
- at the time the new employee is employed, no other industrial instrument covers the new employee.

Transfer of Entitlements

Generally speaking, where there is a transfer of a business and employees of the old employer are engaged by the purchaser of that business, the new employer will be required to recognize any period of service that the employees have with the old employer as service with the new employer. Certain exemptions may apply. Buyers of businesses should seek specific advice on this issue in any transaction.

Redundancy Entitlements

A transferring employee is not entitled to statutory redundancy pay from their former employer on termination of employment if the new employer recognizes the employee's service with the former employer as service with the new employer.

Further, no redundancy pay is owed when an employee rejects an offer of employment from the new employer that is as favourable as their former position, and that recognizes the continuity of service.

Importantly, the above applies only to statutory redundancy pay. Industrial instruments which contain more generous redundancy pay entitlements will need to be examined in each circumstance to determine whether redundancy pay is payable if there is a transfer of business.

7.3. Acquisition Checklist

The following is a checklist of the most common issues, a purchaser will need to identify and, review in respect of the acquisition of a business:

- identify the entitlements of all employees with reference to relevant industrial instruments and (for senior employees) contracts of employment;
- identify all accrued entitlements of employees in respect of annual leave, personal leave and long service leave;
- determine whether any bonus schemes are in place;
- identify whether any entitlements are owed on a change in ownership;
- ascertain whether senior management is able to resign and compete with the seller, or whether enforceable restraints of trade are in place;
- identify whether intellectual property is adequately protected;
- review independent contractor arrangements;
- determine if there have been any notices for breaches of industrial instruments issued by the relevant government authority;
- determine whether there have been prosecutions and/or investigations for breaches of Work Health and Safety (WHS) laws and request any safety audit reports that have been conducted;
- review health and safety and discrimination policies to assess whether they are adequate;
- investigate whether there has been any safety or employment litigation;
- ensure that all WorkCover insurance premiums have been paid and that the claims history is acceptable;
- identify any agreements that are being negotiated/wage claims in progress;
- identify lost time due to industrial disputes.

7.4. Sale of a Business

In respect of a sale of a business, the seller should be concerned to ensure that as few entitlements as possible have to be paid. Generally, it is possible to avoid paying redundancy pay and compensation for accrued annual leave and long service leave entitlements where the new employer agrees to employ employees on materially the same terms and recognizes continuity of service.

If the sale is by way of shares, the above issues do not arise.

7.5. Sale Checklist

The seller should identify and review all requirements to make payments to former employees, including:

- termination of employment or redundancy procedures/policies;
- contracts of employment;

- bonus policies;
- industrial instruments; and
- in the event that there is a sale of shares, identify whether there are any superannuation liabilities which are unfunded.

8. USE OF ALTERNATIVE WORKFORCES: INDEPENDENT CONTRACTORS, CONTRACT EMPLOYEES AND TEMPORARY OR LEASED WORKERS

8.1. Overview

Independent contractors and contract workers are engaged by many companies in Australia to provide flexibility in their labour arrangements. The FW Act contains provisions which prohibit employers from misrepresenting an employment relationship as an independent contractor relationship or from making a statement, which is known to be false, in order to persuade a person to enter into an independent contractor arrangement.

Independent contractors may also be able to make a claim under the *Independent Contractors Act 2006* (Cth) on the basis that their contract is unfair or harsh. In practice, claims under this legislation are unusual.

8.2. Independent Contractors

8.2.1. Definition

In Australia, an independent contractor performs services based on a contract for services rather than a contract of service. Prior to 2022, there was no uniform test applied by the courts to determine whether an individual was an employee or an independent contractor. Courts and tribunals would consider the 'totality of the relationship' between the parties, examining various 'indicia', that extended beyond the terms of the written agreement.

However, this all changed following the High Court's decisions in *Construction, Forestry, Maritime, Mining and Energy Union v. Personnel Contracting Pty Ltd* [2022] HCA 1 (9 February 2022) (*Personnel Contracting*), and *ZG Operations Australia Pty Ltd v. Jamsek* [2022] HCA 2 (9 February 2022) (*Jamsek*).

Personnel Contracting and *Jamsek* stand for the proposition that where there is a valid and comprehensive written independent contractor agreement between the parties, that document is solely determinative of the parties' relationship, unless there is a reason to argue that the contract is invalid or should be set aside. Consequently, absent some unconscionable conduct or another basis for arguing that the relevant agreement is invalid, workers engaged by such agreements will be regarded as independent contractors at law.

8.2.2. Creating the Relationship

In order to ensure that the relationship is that of a principal and independent contractor, a written contract should be entered into which specifies that the individual is an independent contractor rather than an employee. The written contract should also specify the services that are to be provided.

8.2.3. Compensation

The written contract should set out how and when the independent contractor will be compensated for the provision of the services and address any issues in respect of invoices and tax. The written contract should also specify that the independent contractor will be responsible for all wages and other employment-related entitlements of the independent contractor's employees.

8.2.4. Other Terms and Conditions

Typically, a written contract with an independent contractor will also deal with matters such as the duration of the contract, the time for performance of the services, reporting arrangements, the provision of materials, exclusivity, confidentiality, intellectual property and moral rights, termination, taxes, insurance and indemnities.

8.3. Contract Workers

8.3.1. Definition

A contract worker or 'on-hire' is typically employed by a labour hire company, and the services of the worker are provided by the labour hire company to another company under a commercial arrangement between the two companies.

Contract workers or 'on-hire' are generally used to manage fluctuations in workflows. However, to the extent that work previously performed by employees of the employer is 'outsourced', this may give rise to a 'transfer of business' within the meaning of the FW Act, which could trigger the requirement to make payments under the industrial instruments which apply to any employees who subsequently become employed by the labour hire company (*see* section 7). Further, if after a period of time, an employee is required to perform the same work for the employer through a labour hire company, there are risks that the employee will be considered to have remained an employee of the employer rather than of the labour hire company.

The company and the labour hire company should have a written agreement that specifies the rights and obligations of both parties.

In addition, labour hire licensing schemes have been introduced in a number of jurisdictions in Australia in response to concerns regarding the exploitation of certain labour hire workers. In general, the labour hire licensing schemes require that labour hire providers must have a licence to operate in the jurisdiction, those who use labour hire services must only engage licensed providers and reports must be provided on labour hire activities.

8.3.2. No Obligation to Provide Salary, Wages and Benefits

Any payments or wages to the contract workers should be made by the labour hire company, and the written arrangement should specify that the labour hire company is responsible for all wages, benefits and employment-related entitlements (including any payments relating to termination or redundancy).

8.3.3. No Right to Continued Work

Contract workers will generally have no right to continued engagement with the company to which they have been assigned. The company can simply terminate its agreement with the labour hire company in accordance with the terms of that agreement. Their ongoing employment must be managed by the labour hire company in accordance with the terms of their employment with the labour hire company. Often the contract between the company and the labour hire company will place restrictions on the ability to offer employment to the contract workers.

8.4. Leased Workers

There is no relevant distinction between leased workers and contract workers in Australia.

8.5. Checklist of Dos and Don'ts

- Ensure that arrangements with independent contractors and labour hire companies are set out in a written agreement, which specifies the nature of the relationship and the rights and obligations of all parties.
- Do not misrepresent an employment relationship as an independent contractor relationship, or otherwise make false statements designed to persuade individuals to enter into an independent contractor relationship. For example, do not tell a person that they would be better off under a contracting arrangement if this clearly is not the case.
- When outsourcing or employing an individual from a labour hire entity, seek legal advice as to whether the 'transfer of business' provisions of the FW Act applies.
- Ensure that labour hire companies have appropriate licences in place for the jurisdiction in which they operate.

9. OBLIGATION TO BARGAIN COLLECTIVELY WITH TRADE UNIONS: EMPLOYEES' RIGHT TO STRIKE AND A COMPANY'S RIGHT TO CONTINUE BUSINESS OPERATIONS

9.1. Overview of Unions' Right to Organize

Unions played a central role in Australia's traditional conciliation and arbitration system of industrial regulation. Registered trade unions obtained de facto rights of 'recognition' from employers, through the ability to serve a 'log of claims' that formed the basis for the creation of an 'industrial dispute' which could be settled by the federal industrial tribunal making an 'award' (a legally enforceable document regulating wages and other employment conditions). Unions also enjoyed significant organizational rights under the conciliation and arbitration system, including legalized 'closed shop' arrangements, and 'rights of entry' to workplaces to ensure compliance with awards and for recruitment purposes.

Since the early 1990s, there has been a shift away from the traditional conciliation and arbitration system towards a system of 'enterprise bargaining'. Although initially, unions were the main conduit for the negotiation of collective or 'enterprise agreements', the role of unions in enterprise bargaining was subsequently reduced through the introduction of non-union agreements and (later) individual statutory agreements, known as 'Australian Workplace Agreements' (AWAs). The Coalition Government (1996–2007) introduced AWAs and placed limits upon many of the former guarantees of 'union security' under Australian law. For example, freedom of association rights was matched by legal protection of the right *not* to associate (thus ending the closed shop), and new requirements were imposed on union officials seeking to enter employers' premises for enforcement and recruitment purposes.

The FW Act encourages collective bargaining and gives unions enhanced rights in the bargaining process. Whether these laws will assist Australian unions to reverse their 'membership slide' over the past twenty-five years or so remains to be seen.

9.2. Right of Employees to Join Unions and Overview of Collective Bargaining Framework

Australian employees are entitled, under the FW Act and the *Fair Work (Registered Organisations) Act 2009* (Cth) (FWRO Act), to join any union that has the right under its rules to cover the type of work being (or to be) performed by the relevant employee(s). The FWRO Act regulates various aspects of the operation, accountability and democratic control of registered unions (and employer associations). Unions register with FWC.

With effect from 1 July 2009, the FW Act established a system of collective bargaining based on the principles of 'majority employee support' and 'Good Faith Bargaining' (GFB) (*see* section 9.5). This collective bargaining framework applies to most Australian private sector employers, as well as federal public service departments/agencies and all employers in Victoria, the Australian Capital Territory (ACT) and the Northern Territory. Public sector employers in the remaining five states are covered by state legislation.

Another important feature of the collective bargaining scheme under the FW Act is that employees and unions may take 'protected' industrial action in support of claims made in collective bargaining negotiations, and employers can impose retaliatory 'lockouts' which is the employers' form of protected action. 'Protected' industrial action means industrial action that is taken during collective bargaining, which is immune from the legal consequences that can flow from taking industrial action. There are many statutory requirements that must be met before protected action can be taken – including approval of proposed employee/union industrial action by a majority of employees voting in a secret ballot. The effect of amendments made to the FW Act in 2015 and most recently in 2023, with the introduction of the *Fair Work Legislation Amendment (Secure Jobs, Better Pay) Act 2022* (Cth) (SJBP Act), is that a union/employees cannot apply for a protected action ballot order unless:

- the employer has agreed to or initiated bargaining for the enterprise agreement;
- the employer receives a written request to bargain from a bargaining representative (i.e., a union) for a single-enterprise agreement that will replace a previous agreement of this kind, provided that:
  - a single interest employer authorization (SIEA) did not cease to be in operation because of the making of the earlier agreement
  - no more than five years have passed since the nominal expiry date of the former agreement; and
  - the proposed agreement will cover the same or substantially the same group of employees as the earlier agreement.
- a Majority Support Determination (MSD) in relation to the agreement has come into operation;
- a scope order in relation to the agreement has come into operation;
- a supported bargaining authorization in relation to the agreement that specifies the employer has come into operation; or
- an SIEA in relation to the agreement that specifies the employer comes into operation.

As to MSDs and scope orders, *see* section 9.4 below. As to SIEAs, *see* section 9.5 below.

9.3. How Employees Select Unions

Employees may join a union that is constituted to cover their occupation or industry. Unions are then *automatically* entitled to act as the bargaining representative of any of their members who will be covered by a proposed enterprise agreement (unless an employee appoints someone else to act as his/her bargaining representative).

9.4. Pre-election Campaigning

In Australia, the 'majority support' mechanism under the FW Act is used to determine whether a majority of employees in a workplace wish to engage in *collective bargaining*, and (therefore) whether their employer will be compelled to bargain with their bargaining representative(s) (*see* 9.4 above).

Employees (in practice, through their union bargaining representatives) are entitled to seek MSDs from FWC.

Before making an MSD, FWC must be satisfied (among other things) that a majority of employees who will be covered by a proposed enterprise agreement want to bargain.

It should however be noted that due to the SJBP Act reforms, MSDs will become otiose in circumstances where a bargaining representative is able to unilaterally initiate bargaining for a single-enterprise agreement.

The concept of majority support is also key for the granting of an SIEA (*see* section 9.5 below), as a majority of each employer's employees to be covered by the proposed agreement must want to bargain for it.

Disputes about the composition of employee bargaining units (i.e., the group of employees that will be covered by an agreement) can be resolved through applications to FWC for 'scope orders'.

9.5. Multi-employer Bargaining

The SJBP Act made significant amendments to the provisions of the FW Act that address multi-employer bargaining.

As of 6 June 2023, there are three streams available:

(1) SIEA stream – relating to agreements between two or more employers in accordance with an SIEA;
(2) Supported bargaining authorization stream – this stream replaces the previous 'low paid bargaining stream'; and
(3) Cooperative workplaces stream – this stream essentially renames the old voluntary multi-enterprise bargaining stream and retains the requirement that the employer consents to bargaining.

The amendments relating to the SIEA stream are among the most significant industrial relations reforms in decades.

SIEA Stream

There is no longer any requirement that the Minister approves multi-employer bargaining in this stream. Rather, a bargaining representative of an employee may apply to the FWC for an SIEA and nominate multiple employers as a party to a proposed agreement, provided they are not covered by an 'in-term' agreement.

Before granting an application for an SIEA, the FWC must be satisfied with the below matters:

- at least some of the employees to be covered by the proposed multi-enterprise agreement are represented by a union;
- a majority of each employer's employees to be covered by the proposed agreement must want to bargain for it (*see* discussion in section 9.4 above);
- the employers have clearly identifiable common interests, which include considerations as to geographical location, regulatory regime and the

nature of employment (this is presumed to be the case where the employer has fifty or more employees);
- the SIEA is not contrary to the public interest;
- the operations and business activities of each employer must be reasonably comparable with those of the other employers to be covered by the agreement (this is presumed to be the case where the employer has fifty or more employees);
- the employer must not have a written agreement with a relevant union, to bargain for a proposed single-enterprise agreement that would cover the employer and the employees;
- the employer must have at least twenty employees (including part-time employees and regular and systematic casuals).

If satisfied with the above, the FWC retains a limited discretion to exclude an employer from an SIEA if:

- the employer is bargaining in good faith with its employees for a new agreement less than nine months after the nominal expiry of a previous agreement; and
- there is a history of effective bargaining between the employer and its employees.

An employer cannot bargain with its employees for any other kind of agreement while an SIEA that covers it is in operation. Typically, an SIEA will cease operating after 12 months, unless the term is extended by the FWC. Importantly, it is open for employees to take protected industrial action in the course of bargaining negotiations for an SIEA agreement.

Once an SIEA agreement is made, additional employers can be added to the agreement on application by a union. Essentially the same requirements as above apply in this process.

An employer can apply to the FWC to exit from a SIEA agreement, if it is 'no longer appropriate' for it to be covered by the agreement, on the basis that its circumstances have changed.

9.6. Unfair Labour Practices/GFB Obligations

The FW Act does not define 'unfair labour practices'. The FW Act does prohibit the taking of 'adverse action' based on industrial activity (*see* sections 340(1)(a) and (b), 340(2), 341(2)(c)).

The negotiating tactics and conduct of both employer and employee bargaining representatives are, however, governed by the GFB obligations outlined in the FW Act. To comply with the GFB requirements, the bargaining representatives are required to:

- attend and participate in meetings at reasonable times;
- disclose relevant information (but not confidential or commercially sensitive information) in a timely manner;
- respond to proposals made by other bargaining representatives in a timely manner;
- give genuine consideration to the proposals made by other bargaining representatives, and give reasons for the responses made to those proposals;
- refrain from capricious or unfair conduct that undermines freedom of association or collective bargaining;
- recognize and bargain with the other bargaining representatives.

However, the GFB obligations do *not* require a bargaining representative to make concessions during bargaining or to reach an agreement on the terms to be included.

The GFB duties are enforceable through 'bargaining orders', which a bargaining representative may seek from FWC when another representative has failed to comply with any of the GFB obligations. Previously, a party's serious and persistent breaches of bargaining orders could result in a 'serious breach declaration' being made by the FWC, which in turn created a potential pathway for the making of a 'bargaining related workplace determination.'

However, these concepts have been replaced by the SJBP Act reforms, which introduced a new mechanism for compulsory arbitration of enterprise agreements where bargaining negotiations reach an impasse. Under the new framework, a bargaining representative for a proposed single-enterprise agreement, an SIEA agreement or a supported bargaining agreement may apply to the FWC for an 'intractable bargaining declaration' (IB Declaration).

Broadly, the FWC is able to make an IB Declaration when, in addition to other criteria, it is satisfied that there is no 'reasonable prospect of agreement being reached'. After making the IB Declaration, provided the agreement is not reached in any 'post-declaration negotiation period' which the FWC may mandate, the FWC must make an 'intractable bargaining workplace determination', which sets the terms of the relevant agreement.

9.7. Relocation of Work/Shutdown of Business

Restructuring issues may form the subject of enterprise agreement negotiations under the FW Act. Employers may also have legal obligations to inform and consult with their employees/unions about proposed restructures and redundancies, under applicable awards or enterprise agreements and/or specific provisions of the FW Act (*see* section 6).

9.8. Checklist of Dos and Don'ts

- Employers should be aware of the unions that cover, or have the right to cover, the work performed by employees in their workplace or enterprise. These are the unions that are likely to seek to organize and represent employees in collective bargaining under the FW Act.
- Employers should be aware of the risk of multi-employer bargaining and consider the protections afforded by single-enterprise employer agreements.
- Employers need to consider the GFB obligations, the consequences of breaching them and the new intractable bargaining provisions in formulating and implementing bargaining and negotiation strategies.
- Case law emanating from FWC to date indicates that 'hard bargaining', some forms of direct communication with employees, and implementing restructures during bargaining may all be legitimate actions for employers to take. The FWC may, however, make a bargaining order to require an employer to put a genuine offer to the union, rather than withdraw from discussions. The state of the case law is fluid, and contrary positions on these and other matters may soon be arrived at by FWC. Employers should seek legal advice in preparation for, and during the course of, bargaining.

10. WORKING CONDITIONS: HOURS OF WORK AND PAYMENT OF WAGES – BY STATUTE OR COLLECTIVE AGREEMENT

10.1. Overview of Wages and Hour Laws in Australia

In Australia, employees are entitled to the conditions imposed by the NES (*see* section 11).

Under the NES, a maximum of thirty-eight-hour week applies for full-time employees. However, employees may be requested to work reasonable additional hours. An employee can refuse to work additional hours if they are unreasonable. In determining whether additional hours are reasonable or unreasonable, a range of factors must be taken into account, including any risk to employee health and safety from working additional hours, the employee's personal circumstances (including family responsibilities), the needs of the enterprise and the nature of the employee's role, and the employee's level of responsibility.

Modern awards supplement and operate in conjunction with the NES, adding industry-specific detail to the statutory standards. For example, the NES does not set a maximum duration for each shift; however, a modern award or enterprise agreement or contract of employment may set out maximum shift duration or impose other restrictions, such as overtime compensation. Significantly, modern awards also provide minimum wage entitlements for most employees in the national workplace system.

In addition to the NES and the modern awards, an employee's hours of work and payment of wages may be regulated by the terms of an employee's contract of employment or relevant industrial instrument (such as an enterprise agreement), provided that these do not contravene the terms of the NES or an applicable modern award.

10.2. Minimum Wage

Since 1 January 2010, the NES has established the minimum wage system so that:

- for award-covered employees, minimum wages are guaranteed under modern awards; and
- for award-free employees, minimum wages are guaranteed under the national minimum wage order. As of 1 July 2022, this minimum rate was AUD 21.38 per hour.

Employees covered by an enterprise agreement will receive the pay rates specified in the agreement. However, those rates must at least equal the base rate of pay under the applicable modern award, and the rates in the award will be no less than the national minimum.

10.3. Overtime

Overtime is usually defined as work performed by an employee for his or her employer outside or in addition to the hours fixed by an award or agreement as 'ordinary hours' of work. 'Ordinary hours' are often defined to be up to thirty-eight hours a week, worked within a certain spread of hours (e.g., for non-shift workers – between 6 am and 6 pm from Monday to Friday).

An applicable award, agreement or contract may indicate that overtime is voluntary so that an employee can be asked but not compelled to work extra hours. On the other hand, an applicable award, agreement or contract may require an employee to work overtime when asked to do so. Typically, even when an employee is required to work overtime, the award, agreement or contract allows an employee to refuse to work 'unreasonable' overtime.

Upon working 'overtime', employees may be entitled to a penalty payment, for example, double time for working on a Sunday. However, there is no standard entitlement to overtime rates of pay. The entitlement only arises where a provision is made for overtime rates in an award, an agreement or a contract between the employer and the employee.

10.4. Meal and Rest Periods

Modern awards and other industrial instruments commonly require the provision of meal breaks or other rest breaks. There is no standard across all industries, and each award should be reviewed to assess when such breaks are required.

10.5. Deductions from Wages

Under the FW Act, an employer is allowed to make a deduction from an employee's pay if one of the following applies:

(1) the employee has authorized the deduction in writing (with the amount of the deduction specified), and the deduction is principally for the employee's benefit; or
(2) the deduction is authorized by the employee in accordance with:
  (a) an industrial instrument;
  (b) a modern award;
  (c) an FWC order;
  (d) a law or an order of a court.

However, a term in an enterprise agreement, modern award, industrial instrument or contract of employment that allows for deductions has no effect if:

- the deduction is directly or indirectly for the benefit of the employer and is unreasonable;
- the employee is under the age of 18 and the employee's parent or guardian has not authorized the deduction in writing.

The Fair Work Regulations 2009 (Cth) provides that certain deductions are to be treated as reasonable, for example, to recover costs incurred through private use by the employee of a credit card, mobile phone or petrol for a vehicle that has been provided by the employer.

In accordance with the above conditions, an employee may request a deduction for various reasons. The typical types of deductions from wages sought by employees are salary-sacrificing arrangements (e.g., salary sacrificing for superannuation, car or computer).

10.6. Garnishment

A court can issue an order to garnish an employee's wages (typically to satisfy a judgment against the employee). The order will usually specify the amount of money to be withdrawn from the employee's pay for a specified period.

10.7. Exemptions to Wage and Hour Laws

Exemptions to Wage Laws

Employers are not able to 'opt-out' of modern award coverage. However, while a modern award will 'cover' employees in a particular industry, it will not always 'apply' to those employees. Rights and obligations under an award will only arise where the relevant instrument 'applies'.

Guarantees of Annual Earnings (High-Income Employees)

A modern award will not apply while an employee is a 'high-income employee'; that is, an employee in relation to whom a 'Guarantee of Annual Earnings' (GAE) above the 'high-income threshold' (currently AUD 162,000 per annum, but indexed annually) is in effect.

There are a number of technical requirements for making an effective GAE. Specific advice should be sought to access this exemption.

Individual Flexibility Arrangements

In circumstances where a modern award applies, its terms may be varied by an Individual Flexibility Arrangement (IFA).

All modern awards include a flexibility term that allows an employer to enter into an IFA with an individual employee, varying the effect of certain terms of the modern award in order to meet the genuine needs of the employer and employee.

The scope of an IFA and how an IFA may be made will depend on the 'enabling provision' in the modern award. However, the model flexibility clause that is included in most modern awards allows an employer and an employee to agree to enter into an IFA in relation to:

- arrangements for when work is performed;
- overtime rates;
- penalty rates;
- allowances; and
- leave loading (which is an additional payment or loading that an employer may be required to pay an employee when they take annual leave).

Modern awards now provide for the termination of IFAs by either party upon the giving of thirteen weeks' notice.

The FW Act imposes conditions in order to implement IFAs; for example, there must be a genuine agreement between the employer and employee, the agreement must be in writing and the employer must ensure that the employee is better off overall under the IFA than if the IFA was not implemented.

10.8. Child Labour

The federal workplace relations laws in Australia provide that employers can still be covered by state and territory laws on 'child labour'. Accordingly, in each state and territory in Australia, there are laws that place limits on the employment of children or minors, for example:

- New South Wales – *Children and Young Persons (Care and Protection) Act 1998* (CYP Act).
- Victoria – *Child Employment Act 2003.*
- Queensland – *Child Employment Act 2006.*
- South Australia – Education and Children's Services Act 2019 and *Children and Young People (Safety Act) 2017.*
- Western Australia – *School Education Act 1999* and *Children and Community Services Act 2004.*
- Tasmania – *Education Act 2016.*
- ACT – *Children and Young People Act 2008* and *Children and Young People (Employment) Standards 2011 (No 1).*
- Northern Territory – *Care and Protection of Children Act 2007* and *Education Act 2016.*

Each of the Acts above imposes regulations on the employment of children. For example, in New South Wales, the CYP Act governs the employment of children under the age of 15 or, in the case of employment as a model, under 16 years of age. The CYP Act also provides that certain types of employers require authorization before employing a child, that is, depending on the type of employment, a person under 15 or 16 years of age. Activities that require authorization include:

– taking part in entertainment or exhibition;
– taking part in a performance which is recorded for use in a subsequent entertainment or exhibition;
– offering anything for sale door to door.

Furthermore, the CYP Act provides additional protection so that children may be removed from unlawful employment at any place, and a person who causes or allows a child to take part in any employment in the course of which the child's physical or emotional well-being is at risk is guilty of an offence, and monetary penalties may be imposed.

10.9. Record-Keeping Requirements

Under the FW Act, an employer's records must:

– be easy to access;
– be written in English;
– be kept for seven years;
– not be altered unless for the purpose of correcting an error; and
– not be false or misleading to the employer's knowledge.

10.9.1. Information That Must Be Maintained

The FW Act and Regulations set out that employers must keep records in respect of each employee about matters including:

– basic employment details, such as the name of the employer and employee, the nature of their employment (full-time, part-time or casual), the date the employee started employment if the employee is permanent or temporary;
– pay;
– overtime hours;
– averaging arrangements;
– leave entitlements (including leave taken, leave balance and details of any written agreement to cash out leave);
– superannuation contributions;
– where applicable, termination of employment details (e.g., name of the person who terminated the employment and how the termination took place); and
– IFAs and guarantees of annual earnings.

Specifically, in relation to an employee's pay, an employer must keep a record that specifies:

- the rate of remuneration paid to the employee;
- the gross and net amounts paid to the employee;
- any deductions made from the gross amount paid to the employee;
- if the employee is a casual or irregular part-time employee who is guaranteed a rate of pay by reference to a period of time worked, the record must set out the hours worked by the employee;
- if the employee is entitled to be paid an incentive-based payment, a bonus, a loading, a monetary penalty rate, monetary allowance or separately identifiable entitlement, details of such payment.

In addition to the above, employers are required to record specific information on an employee's payslip.

In respect of hours, an employer's records must include:

(1) where a penalty rate or loading must be paid for overtime hours actually worked by an employee:
   (a) the number of overtime hours worked by the employee during each day; or
   (b) when the employee started and ceased working overtime hours.
(2) where an employer and employee agree in writing to an average of the employee's hours of work, a copy of the averaging agreement.

Employee records are private and confidential, and they can usually only be accessed by the employee, employer and relevant payroll staff. However, Fair Work Inspectors and union officials may be able to access employees' records to determine if there has been a contravention of Commonwealth workplace laws.

10.9.2. Records That Must Be Retained

The FW Act set out that an employer must make and keep an employee's records (as set out above) for seven years.

Further, modern awards that contain annualized wage provisions have recently been varied to provide that an employer must, for each employee covered by an annualized wage arrangement, keep a record of:

- the starting and finishing times of work; and
- any unpaid breaks taken.

This record must be signed by the employee or acknowledged as correct in writing (including by electronic means) by the employee, each pay period or roster cycle.

10.9.3. Failure to Maintain Required Records

A penalty can be imposed on an employer who fails to comply with the record-keeping requirements set out under the FW Act (currently, the maximum penalty is AUD 165,000 per contravention and up to AUD 825,000 for a 'serious contravention'). Further, an employer who fails to comply with the record-keeping requirements of the FW Act will bear the onus of disproving any allegation that they contravened relevant provisions of the FW Act (e.g., underpayment of an employee).

10.10. Reductions in Compensation Caused by Economic Downturn

An employer has no implied right to unilaterally vary the contract terms in response to an economic downturn since contractual obligations can only be varied by mutual agreement.

An employer and an employee can mutually agree to vary the terms of employment. For example, due to an economic downturn, the parties may agree that the employee will only work four days per week in exchange for a reduced salary. However, the reduced terms and conditions of employment cannot be reduced below the minimum conditions imposed by statute or under another instrument, such as a relevant modern award or enterprise agreement.

10.11. Checklist Dos and Don'ts

- Ensure that employees are paid in accordance with the terms of any applicable modern award, enterprise agreement or contract of employment, and receive minimum entitlements in accordance with the NES.
- Ensure that any deductions from an employee's wages are authorized by the employee (in writing) or the deduction is authorized by an industrial instrument, modern award, law or order.
- Check the relevant award labour laws before employing a child (these laws vary between each state and territory in Australia).
- Ensure that all employee records are made and kept for a period of at least seven years.

11. OTHER WORKING CONDITIONS AND BENEFITS: BY STATUTE, COLLECTIVE AGREEMENTS OR COMPANY POLICY

11.1. Introduction

Employees covered by the national workplace relations system (*see* section 1) are entitled to the working conditions and benefits provided under the NES (*see* section 11.2). The NES is contained in the FW Act.

Many employees will also be entitled to the benefits contained in industry-specific or occupation-specific modern awards (*see* section 11.3). Modern awards are instruments made under the FW Act by the industrial umpire, FWC. Generally, managerial employees and employees in certain professions will be excluded from the operation of modern awards.

Other statutes, such as those regulating superannuation, workers' compensation, paid parental leave (PPL) or equal employment opportunity, also confer benefits on most employees (*see* section 11.6).

Collective (enterprise) agreements may improve on the benefits contained in the NES and modern awards and may also contain a wide range of other benefits (*see* section 11.4). Employees are not entitled to take industrial action prior to the nominal expiry date of a collective (enterprise) agreement.

A number of companies also provide enhanced employee benefits (such as bonuses or health insurance) via company policy (*see* section 12). Where this is done, it is often prudent for the employer to ensure that such policies are not inadvertently incorporated into contracts of employment, thereby giving rise to contractual benefits that cannot be varied without employee consent.

11.2. National Employment Standards

In addition to regulating hours of work (*see* section 10), the NES provides for and regulates the employee benefits listed below. The NES is eleven minimum standards. Except as specified in the FW Act, the NES cannot be limited or abrogated by a modern award, collective agreement or contract of employment.

11.2.1. Right to Request Flexible Working Arrangements

An employee with at least twelve months' continuous service who has responsibility for the care of a child of school age or younger (certain other categories of employee, such as a carer as defined in legislation, an employee with a disability or who is aged 55 or over) may request flexible working arrangements from their employer to assist with those caring responsibilities. The employer must respond to the request within twenty-one days and is permitted to refuse the request on 'reasonable business grounds'. Reforms to the FW Act which commenced in 2023 now entitle employees to dispute a refusal by their employer to grant a flexible working arrangement at the FWC.

11.2.2. Right to Request Casual Conversion

A casual employee is entitled to access to transition to permanent full-time or permanent part-time status in some circumstances.

An employer is required to offer permanent status to a casual employee if that employee has worked for the employer for twelve months, has worked regular hours for six months of those months, and those hours could continue if the employee was a permanent employee. From 27 September 2021, an employee will also be able to request conversion to become a permanent employee providing: they have been employed by the employer for at least twelve months, they have worked a regular pattern of hours in the past six months on an ongoing basis, those regular hours could continue as a permanent employee without significant changes, the employee has not refused a previous offer to become a permanent employee in the past six months, the employer has not told them in the past six months that they will not offer casual conversion on reasonable grounds, and the employer has not already refused a request from the employee to become a permanent employee based on reasonable grounds in the past six months.

11.2.3. Parental Leave

Each employee who has completed at least twelve months of continuous service is entitled to twelve months' unpaid parental leave in connection with the birth or adoption of a child. Other than an eight-week period of 'concurrent leave', the leave may not be taken concurrently by both parents.

A parent may request up to twelve months' additional leave from their employer. If such leave is granted by the employer, the other parent's entitlement to leave is reduced by an equivalent amount.

The NES also provides a female employee with unpaid special maternity leave if the employee suffers a pregnancy-related illness or the pregnancy ends after twelve weeks (other than by the birth of a living child). A female employee is also entitled to be transferred to a safer job during her pregnancy if it is unsafe for her to remain in her regular job. If there is no safe job available, the employee is entitled to paid leave.

Parental leave entitlements also extend to employees who are not covered by the national workplace relations system.

Separate legislation deals with PPL as set out in section 11.7.

11.2.4. Annual Leave

Employees (other than casual employees) are entitled to four weeks of paid leave per year. Shift workers (as defined in the FW Act, modern relevant award or collective agreement) are entitled to an extra week's annual leave. Limited provision is made available for cashing out annual leave as set out in the FW Act, relevant modern award or collective agreement. Untaken annual leave accrues from year to year and is paid out upon termination of employment.

Subject to the provisions of any applicable modern award, employers may direct employees to take annual leave at particular times (e.g., a Christmas shutdown of the business or where the employee has accrued excessive annual leave).

11.2.5. Personal Carer's Leave and Compassionate Leave

An employee (other than a casual employee) is entitled to ten days' paid personal/carer's leave per year which may be used where the employee is unable to work due to illness or injury or where the employee needs to care for a member of the employee's immediate family or household due to illness, injury or unexpected emergency (carer's leave).

An employee is also entitled to two days unpaid carer's leave for each occasion when it is required, and the employee has exhausted their paid leave entitlement. Casual employees are also entitled to two days unpaid carer's leave on each occasion it is required.

All employees are entitled to two days' compassionate leave on each occasion of the death or serious illness or injury of a member of the employee's household or immediate family. This is unpaid leave in the case of casual employees and paid leave in all other cases. Employees must provide reasonable notice and evidence of the need to take these various forms of leave.

In February 2023, a new entitlement providing for ten days of paid family and domestic violence leave in a twelve-month period was inserted into the NES. The leave is available in full upfront for all employees but does not roll over from year to year if not used. Employees of a small business employer will be able to access this leave from 1 August 2023 and may take unpaid family and domestic violence leave in the meantime.

11.2.6. Community Service Leave

An employee engaged in certain types of community service activity (including jury duty and voluntary emergency management activities) is entitled to be absent from their employment for a reasonable period to engage in that activity.

Where an employee performs jury duty, the employee is entitled to be paid the difference between the employee's usual base rate of pay and the amount that they receive from the government for the performance of jury duty. Under Commonwealth law, only the first ten days of jury duty are required to be paid. However, legislation in some states (such as Victoria and Queensland) requires employees to be paid for the entire duration of jury service.

11.2.7. Long Service Leave

Long service leave is leave which recognizes a significant period of employment with one employer. For example, in some states, employees are entitled to two months of paid leave after ten years of service. Under current transitional arrangements, employees may be entitled to the benefit of long-service leave provisions contained in existing awards, agreements or state long-service leave legislation.

11.2.8. Public Holidays

Employees are entitled to eight national public holidays plus such other days as are declared under state or territory law. An employee is entitled to be absent from work on a public holiday, but an employer may reasonably request an employee to work. An employee may reasonably refuse that request. The FW Act contains a list of criteria which are to be taken into account for determining whether a request or a refusal is reasonable, for example, the employee's personal circumstances and whether the employee would be entitled to receive overtime/penalty payments.

11.2.9. Notice of Termination

Most employees are entitled to the following minimum periods of notice of termination (or payment in lieu of that notice) based on their period of continuous service:

Employee's Period of Continuous Service with the Employer at the End of the Day the Notice Is Given	*Period of Notice (or Pay in Lieu)*
Not more than 1 year	1 week
More than 1 year but not more than 3 years	2 weeks
More than 3 years but not more than 5 years	3 weeks
More than 5 years	4 weeks
Increase the period of notice by 1 week, if the employee is over 45 and has completed at least 2 years of service	

Certain types of employees are not entitled to minimum notice of termination of their employment. Such employees include those whose employment is terminated for serious misconduct, fixed-term employees or casual employees.

This entitlement also extends to employees who are not covered by the national workplace relations system.

11.2.9.1. Redundancy Pay

An employee whose employment is terminated on the ground of redundancy is entitled to redundancy pay depending on their period of continuous service with the employer (as to redundancy pay, *see* section 6).

11.3. Modern Awards

An employer is required to comply with a modern award to the extent that it applies to its employees. A modern award might be expressed to cover all employers in a particular industry or all employees who perform in a particular occupation.

Multiple modern awards may operate within an employer's business. Rules contained within modern awards are intended to avoid the coverage of an employee by more than one modern award.

Modern awards may only deal with the following matters:

- Minimum wages;
- Type of employment (such as full-time, part time or casual employment);
- Arrangements for when work is performed (e.g., hours of work, rostering and rest breaks);
- Overtime rates;
- Penalty rates (e.g., for employees working shifts or on weekends or public holidays);
- Annualized wage arrangements;
- Allowances;
- Leave, leave loadings and arrangements for taking leave;
- Superannuation;
- Procedures for consultation, representation and dispute settlement;
- Matters permitted by the NES for inclusion in modern awards.

Modern awards must also contain a provision that allows an employer and an individual employee to enter into an arrangement (an 'IFA') that allows for the modification of certain terms of the award to the extent permitted by the award.

With effect from 1 December 2018, a model term for requests for flexible working arrangements was inserted into all modern awards, which supplements the rights of employees to request flexible working arrangements under the NES (*see* section 11.2). Under the model term, employers are required to provide reasoning for any refusal and to assess alternative arrangements where the request is denied.

A term has also been inserted in the majority of modern awards which provides the right for casual employees to request full-time or part-time employment status.

11.4. Collective Agreements

Collective (enterprise) agreements may contain terms about any of the following matters:

- matters pertaining to the relationship between the employer and the employer's employees;
- matters pertaining to the relationship between the employer and a union that will be covered by the agreement;
- deductions from wages for any purpose authorized by an employee; and
- how the collective agreement will operate.

It is unlawful to include certain terms in a collective agreement. If such terms are included, FWC must refuse to approve the agreement. Unlawful terms are terms that:

- would result in a breach of anti-discrimination laws;
- would infringe on an employee's workplace rights (including the right to freedom of association);
- would confer unfair dismissal entitlements on employees before they have met the statutory qualifying period (as to unfair dismissal, *see* section 5);
- modify unfair dismissal entitlements to the detriment of employees;
- are inconsistent with the statutory rules regarding industrial action and strike pay; or
- confer on unions more generous rights of entry to workplaces for the purposes specified in the FW Act.

While in operation, a collective agreement applies to the exclusion of a modern award. However, except in exceptional circumstances, FWC may only approve a collective agreement if it leaves employees better off overall than they would be under the modern award.

11.5. Enforcement of the NES, Modern Awards and Collective Agreements

Where an employer fails to comply with the NES, a modern award or a collective agreement, any of the following may commence civil penalty proceedings against the employer:

- an affected employee;
- an inspector; or
- a union (if the union is entitled to represent the industrial interests of an affected employee).

Where an employer is found to have contravened the NES, a modern award or a collective agreement, the relevant court may order:

- an injunction to prevent, stop or remedy the effects of a contravention;
- compensation for the loss that a person has suffered as a result of the contravention;
- reinstatement (e.g., if the employee's employment has been terminated in breach of the NES, modern award or collective agreement);
- payment of a pecuniary penalty (a maximum of AUD 82,500 in the case of a corporation or AUD 825,000 in the case of 'serious contravention').

11.6. General Protections

The FW Act also protects employees and prospective employees from 'adverse action' taken by their employer or prospective employer in connection with a 'workplace right'.

The provisions also apply to principals and independent contractors.

'Adverse action' includes dismissing an employee; injuring an employee in his or her employment; altering the position of the employee to the employee's prejudice; discriminating against an employee; refusing to employ a prospective employee; or discriminating against a prospective employee in the terms and conditions upon which employment is offered.

The protection prohibits an employer or prospective employer from taking such adverse action against an employee or prospective employee for a number of reasons, including:

- because the employee or prospective employee has a workplace right; has or has not exercised a workplace right; or proposes to, proposes not to, or at any time proposed to or proposed not to exercise a workplace right;
- to prevent the employee or prospective employee from exercising a workplace right;
- because of the employee's or prospective employee's industrial affiliations or industrial activity; or
- because of the employee's or prospective employee's race, colour, sex, sexual preference, age, physical or mental disability, marital status, family or carer's responsibilities, pregnancy, religion, political opinion, national extraction, social origin or temporary absence from work because of certain illnesses or injuries (*see* section 17).

A person will have a 'workplace right' if they:

- are entitled to the benefit or a workplace instrument (such as a modern award or enterprise agreement), a workplace law, or an order made by an industrial body;
- have a role or responsibility under a workplace instrument, workplace law or an order made by an industrial body;
- are able to initiate or participate in a process or proceedings under a workplace law or workplace instrument;
- are able to make a complaint or enquiry to a person or body who has the capacity under a workplace law to seek compliance with that workplace law or a workplace instrument; or
- are able to make a complaint or enquiry in relation to their employment.

Employers are also prohibited from:

- coercing an employee or prospective employee to exercise or not exercise their workplace rights, or to exercise them in a particular way;
- exercising undue influence or pressure on an employee in relation to an agreement or arrangement made under the NES, a modern award or an enterprise agreement; an IFA; a GAE; or in relation to deductions from amounts payable to an employee for their work; and

– knowingly or recklessly making a false or misleading representation about a person's workplace rights, the exercise of a person's workplace rights, or the effect of exercising a person's workplace rights.

Where an employer is found to have contravened these protections under the FW Act, the relevant court may order:

– an injunction to prevent, stop or remedy the effects of the contravention;
– compensation for the loss that a person has suffered as a result of the contravention (which is uncapped);
– reinstatement if the adverse action includes a dismissal; or
– payment of a pecuniary penalty (a maximum of AUD 82,500 in the case of a corporation).

11.7. Other Statutory Benefits

Both Commonwealth and state or territory legislation may confer additional benefits on employees. A key employee benefit is compulsory superannuation, which is a retirement income scheme established under Commonwealth legislation.

The effect of that legislation is generally to require employers to contribute (currently) 10.5% (increasing to 11% as of 1 July 2023) of an employee's salary or wages to the employee's choice of superannuation fund (subject to a 'maximum contribution base'). An employee may generally only access their superannuation upon retirement. There is a range of minor exceptions to the requirement to make contributions and to the requirement to offer a choice of fund.

Employers who fail to meet their superannuation obligations will be subject to substantial additional charges.

Paid Parental Leave

The *Paid Parental Leave Scheme Act 2010* (*PPLS Act*) establishes an entitlement to parental leave pay for eligible working parents of children born or adopted on or after 1 January 2011. The entitlement is fully funded by the Federal Government and is designed to complement any existing employment entitlements, such as those set out under the NES (*see* section 11.2).

Under the scheme, eligible working parents may access up to eighteen weeks of government-funded parental leave pay at the rate of the National Minimum Wage (*see* section 10.2).

To be eligible for parental leave pay, a person must:

(a) satisfy the 'work test'(essentially setting minimum requirements for paid work (including paid leave) to be completed prior to the leave period) (set out in Part 2–3 Division 3 of the PPLS Act);

(b) satisfy the ‘income test’ (set out in Part 2–3 Division 4 of the PPLS Act);
(c) satisfy the ‘Australian residency test’ (set out in Part 2–3 Division 5 of the PPLS Act);
(d) be the child’s primary carer;
(e) not have returned to work.

A person is required to lodge a claim for parental leave pay with the Department of Human Services for determination (referred to as a ‘payability determination’) and will be entitled to payment if a payability determination is made in their favour. The determination must also set out the period in which payment is to be provided to the person (PPL Period) up to the eighteen-week cap.

During the PPL Period, parental leave pay is payable in instalments by either a person’s employer or the Secretary of the Department of Human Services. An employer is only required to pay an instalment to a person if the Secretary has made an employer determination which has come into force and has provided sufficient payment to the employer for funding the instalment. Matters may be referred to the FWO for investigation if an employer fails to comply with any payment obligations.

Parental leave pay ceases on the expiry of the PPL Period or if the person returns to work, whichever is earlier.

Changes commencing on 1 July 2023 will extend paid parental leave from eighteen weeks to twenty weeks, with two weeks reserved on a ‘use it or lose it’ basis for each claimant. Parents who are single at the time of their claim will be able to access the full twenty weeks.

Other key changes include a $350,000 family income limit, under which families can be assessed if they do not meet the individual income test and expanding eligibility requirements to allow an eligible father or partner to receive parental leave pay regardless of whether the birth parent meets the income test, residency requirements or is serving a newly arrived resident’s waiting period.

As indicated above, these laws are regularly subject to change as the Federal Government implements changes to the scheme. Accordingly, advice should be sought for a particular individual’s circumstances.

11.8. Company Policies

Company policies may deal with a range of matters such as:

- discrimination and harassment;
- use of information technology;
- paid parental leave;

- WHS matters; or
- prevention of workplace bullying.

Where a company policy is considered to form part of the contract of employment, that policy may only be amended by agreement (in the same way as any other term of the contract of employment).

Commitments by an employer in a company policy to apply fair treatment in the case of workplace grievances carry risk and can result in substantial compensation being payable to an employee if the commitments have not been fulfilled.

11.9. Checklist of Dos and Don'ts

- Update contracts of employment to ensure consistency with the NES.
- Identify modern awards that apply and take steps to ensure compliance.
- Take care to avoid incorporating company policies into contracts of employment.
- Ensure compliance with superannuation obligations.
- Keep complete and accurate records in accordance with statutory requirements in relation to the accrual and taking of entitlements (such as annual leave) under the NES, a modern award or an enterprise agreement (*see* section 26).

12. EMPLOYEE BENEFITS

12.1. Overview

There are many ways that Australian employees can be incentivized. These generally include the following:

- Cash bonuses.
- Employee share plans.
- Profit-sharing arrangements.

Employee share plans are common in Australia and are frequently used by employers as a means of attracting staff and providing incentives for employees. All types of share awards, including share purchase, options, restricted stock and restricted stock units can be offered in Australia. There are securities law issues to consider before granting share awards and filings are usually required. Offering phantom awards is problematic, and specific advice should be obtained before granting them to an employee based in Australia.

Cash bonuses are also commonly used by Australian employers as a means of providing incentives to employees, typically short-term incentives. These can be structured in many ways, for instance, as an annual cash bonus or as part of a profit share scheme. Cash bonuses can be subject to an individual or company performance condition. Termination bonuses for certain company officers and executives may need to be subject to a shareholder vote before they can be paid. Particular types of bonuses may include sign-on bonuses, milestone bonuses (awarded for employees receiving particular targets) or retention bonuses (which are more likely to arise in unusual circumstances such as in a merger, acquisition or when an important project needs to be completed).

12.2. Compensation for Injured Employees

Statutory workers' compensation provides protection to workers and their employers in the event of a work-related injury or disease. Through the workers' compensation system, injured workers may have an entitlement to weekly payments, lump sum payments for permanent impairment (and pain and suffering where applicable), payment of medical bills, provision of legal assistance to pursue a claim and intensive rehabilitation assistance.

Workers' compensation in Australia is regulated by state and territory legislation:

- *Workers Compensation Act 1987* (NSW) and *Workplace Injury Management and Workers Compensation Act 1998* (NSW).
- *Workers Compensation Act 1951* (ACT).
- *Return to Work Act* (NT).
- *Workers' Compensation and Rehabilitation Act 2003* (Qld).
- *Return to Work Act 2014* (SA).
- *Workers Rehabilitation and Compensation Act 1988* (Tas).
- *Workplace Injury Rehabilitation and Compensation Act 2013* (Vic).
- *Workers Compensation and Injury Management Act 1981* (WA).
- *Safety, Rehabilitation and Compensation Act 1988* (Cth) in the Commonwealth jurisdiction.

State and territory legislation provides various benefit structures and cost-reimbursement policies. Further, threshold requirements vary between states and territories, but generally, all employers must have workers' compensation insurance policies in respect of their employees. Employers pay workers' compensation premiums based on the number of workers within the organization and their employee claims history.

Deeming Provisions

Workers' compensation legislation in Victoria,[2] NSW[3] and Queensland[4] contains provisions deeming certain independent contractors to be employees for workers' compensation purposes so that employers are liable for their compensation for work injuries.

The Queensland statute states that in order for the independent contractor to be deemed to be an employee:

- the contractor must be a natural person;
- the work must not be incidental to the contractor's regular business under their own name or a business name; and
- if the contractor is subcontracting or employing other workers, the contractor must still be doing some of the work.

The Victorian statute states that:

- the provision of materials or equipment must not be the principal object of the arrangement;
- at least 80% of the work must be performed by the same individual; and
- at least 80% of the contractor's overall services income must be earned from the principal.

The NSW provision is worded more broadly, encompassing:

- any uninsured person contracted for the execution 'of the whole or any part of any work undertaken by the principal'; but
- excluding persons working under contracts relating to agricultural work if the contractor provides and uses machinery driven by mechanical power for the purposes of that work.

Furthermore, under the NSW legislation, contractors are liable to pay subcontractors' workers' compensation insurance premiums (unless there is a written statement to the contrary).

Benefits

The rate of benefits between states and territories varies. By way of example, in NSW, for the first thirteen weeks that a worker is totally unfit for work, the weekly workers' compensation payments are based on whichever is less than 95% of the worker's pre-injury average weekly earnings or the maximum weekly compensation amount, being a statutory amount that is adjusted in April and October each year. For weeks 14–130 of total incapacity, the weekly workers' compensation payments are based on

2. *Workplace Injury Rehabilitation and Compensation Act 2013* (Vic), Sch. 1, s. 9.
3. *Workers Compensation Act 1987* (NSW), ss 20, 175B.
4. *Workers Compensation Act* 2003 (Qld), s. 11 and Sch. 2.

whichever is less than 80% of the worker's pre-injury average weekly earnings or the maximum weekly compensation amount. The payments are varied again for weeks 131–260. Weekly payments will cease after 260 weeks (five years) unless the level of impairment is greater than 20% and the worker has been assessed as having no work capacity which is likely to continue indefinitely.

Intersection Between Workers' Compensation, Termination of Employment and Discrimination

The FW Act provides that an employer must not dismiss an employee because an employee is temporarily absent from work because of injury or illness. An employee can bring a claim against an employer in the Fair Work Divisions of the Federal Court of Australia or the Federal Circuit Court if the employee is dismissed for this reason. However, an employee will not be 'temporarily absent' and can be dismissed for illness or injury under the FW Act if either:

- the employee's absence extends for more than three months; or
- the total absences of the employee, within a twelve-month period, has been more than three months (whether based on a single illness or injury or separate illnesses or injuries); and
- the employee is not on paid personal carer's leave for the duration of the absence.

NSW employers may be guilty of an offence under the *Workers Compensation Act 1987* (NSW) if the employer dismisses an employee because the worker is unable to work within six months of the date the employee became unfit for work. The majority of state and territory workers' compensation legislation contains similar provisions.

Employers must be careful to properly manage employees on workers' compensation when implementing redundancy programmes so as to ensure mitigation of the risk of discrimination claims. Furthermore, they should carefully consider the position of employees on workers' compensation when considering the implementation of any redeployment or restructuring initiative.

12.3. Checklist of Dos and Don'ts

Employers must ensure that they:

- have a current workers' compensation insurance policy covering all workers;

- display a summary of workers' compensation entitlements, which outlines workers' compensation, what to do if there is an injury and the name and address of the relevant insurance company;
- complete any claim form provided to it by an employee and send it to the relevant insurer;
- pass on any payments to injured workers made to it by its insurer;
- have a comprehensive return-to-work programme that is consistent with the insurance company's injury management programme.

Employers should not:

- dismiss an injured worker on account of his or her injury without carefully considering the circumstances pertaining to the individual;
- try to create a 'one-size-fits-all' injury management/return to work programme. Consider each individual employee's circumstances carefully.

13. COMPANY'S OBLIGATION TO PROVIDE A SAFE AND HEALTHY WORKPLACE

13.1. Overview of Safety and Environmental Laws and Regulations

Each Australian state and territory has its own WHS legislation. In addition, there is a Commonwealth WHS statute which applies, largely to the exclusion of the state and territory WHS statutes, to the Commonwealth government, Commonwealth authorities and non-Commonwealth licensees.

In 2008, the Commonwealth and all states and territories entered into an agreement to enact new WHS legislation to 'harmonize' the WHS laws across Australia. In view of this, Safe Work Australia developed the *Model Work Health and Safety Act* and the *Model Work Health and Safety Regulations*, for adoption across Australia.

The new legislation commenced in New South Wales, Queensland, the ACT, the Northern Territory and the Commonwealth on 1 January 2012 and in Tasmania and South Australia on 1 January 2013. In July 2017, it was announced that Western Australia would develop a bill based on the model WHS laws. After extensive and lengthy debate, the bill was passed by WA Parliament on 3 November 2020 and assented to on 11 November 2020.

The new *Work Health and Safety Act 2020* (WA) took effect from 31 March 2022. This development in WA leaves Victoria as the only jurisdiction not to have harmonized its WHS laws.

As not all states have enacted the harmonized WHS legislation, there remain both significant differences and broad similarities between each state and territory's WHS legislation.

Principal Legislation

The principal WHS Acts and Regulations in each state and territory are set out below:

- *Work Health and Safety Act 2011* (ACT) and *Work Health and Safety Regulation 2011* (ACT) in the ACT.
- *Work Health and Safety Act 2011* (NSW) and *Work Health and Safety Regulation 2017* (NSW) in New South Wales.
- *Work Health and Safety (National Uniform Legislation) Act* (NT) and *Work Health and Safety (National Uniform Legislation) Regulations*(NT) in the Northern Territory.
- *Work Health and Safety Act 2011* (QLD) and *Work Health and Safety Regulation 2011* (QLD) in Queensland.
- *Work Health and Safety Act 2012* (SA) and *Work Health and Safety Regulations 2012* (SA) in South Australia.
- *Work Health and Safety Act 2012* (TAS) and *Work Health and Safety Regulations 2012* (TAS) in Tasmania.
- *Occupational Health and Safety Act 2004* (VIC) and *Occupational Health and Safety Regulations 2017* (VIC) in Victoria.
- *Work Health and Safety Act 2020* (WA) and *Work Health and Safety (General) Regulations 2022.*
- *Work Health and Safety Act 2011* (Cth) and *Work Health and Safety Regulations 2011* (Cth) in the Commonwealth jurisdiction.

The Acts have similar broad objectives. The objectives set out in the *Model Work Health and Safety Act* (as adopted, at the time of writing, in all states and territories except Victoria are to secure the health and safety of workers and workplaces by:

- protecting workers and other persons against harm to their health, safety and welfare through the elimination or minimization of risks arising from work or from specified types of substances or plants;
- providing for fair and effective workplace representation, consultation, cooperation and issue resolution in relation to WHS;
- encouraging unions and employer organizations to take a constructive role in promoting improvements in WHS practices, and assisting persons conducting businesses or undertakings and workers to achieve a healthier and safer working environment;
- promoting the provision of advice, information, education and training in relation to WHS;

- securing compliance with this Act through effective and appropriate compliance and enforcement measures;
- ensuring appropriate scrutiny and review of actions taken by persons exercising powers and performing functions under this Act;
- providing a framework for continuous improvement and progressively higher standards of WHS; and
- maintaining and strengthening the national harmonization of laws relating to WHS and facilitating a consistent national approach to WHS in this jurisdiction.

In broad terms, the Acts prescribe:

- the framework for the operation of the relevant state or territory WHS regulatory enforcement authority;
- the general duties imposed on key duty holders (including in relation to WHS consultation);
- obligations concerning proactive risk management and consultation with workers concerning WHS; and
- the penalties for breach of the general duties.

In developing WHS legislation, all states and territories in Australia have implemented a 'top-down' model. The model has three levels, the principal Act, Regulations made under the Act and Advisory Standards and Industry Codes of Practice. Lower levels provide increasing levels of detail.

Regulations enforce and/or provide technical specifications for specific acts. Regulations have the force of law and their requirements are mandatory. Generally, the principal WHS Regulations in each state and territory of Australia address similar workplace risks, such as:

- hazardous work processes;
- hazardous substances;
- asbestos;
- notification of injuries, illnesses and dangerous events;
- confined spaces; and
- plant and structures.

Standards and Codes are advisory documents that a duty holder may adopt to manage any workplace health and safety risks. Standards and Codes do not, of themselves, have the force of law; however, compliance with WHS laws in relation to a specific subject matter is assisted by following the relevant approved Code. Approved Codes are admissible in court proceedings under the respective WHS legislation. Courts may regard a Code as evidence of what is known about a hazard, risk or control and may rely on the Code in determining what is reasonably practicable in the circumstances to which the Code relates. This relationship means that the role of the Regulations is to set the basic obligations, while the Standards and Codes provide the information necessary to meet these obligations. In this way, the Standards and Codes provide a more detailed and practical guide for duty holders.

Standards and Codes differ from each other in that Standards are designed to detail appropriate health and safety measures which may be common to many different types of industries, whereas Codes typically apply to particular risks that are unique to a specific industry.

13.2. Requirements

WHS laws in Australia are structured around a series of duties. The precise requirements of these duties, and the burden of proof in relation to elements of the offences, vary between jurisdictions.

Generally speaking, the primary obligation is on employers or persons conducting a business or undertaking (depending on the jurisdiction). These duty holders have an obligation to ensure the health, safety and welfare of workers (including contractors, volunteers and those engaged through labour hire organizations) and other persons at work. The obligation to ensure safety is qualified by the concept of what is reasonably practicable for the duty holder to do to discharge its duty.

In addition to the primary obligation, general obligations to prevent risks to health and safety are also imposed upon:

- workers;
- officers of a corporation (which includes directors and senior managers);
- designers, manufacturers and suppliers of plant and substances; and
- occupiers and persons in control of premises used as a place of work and plant used at and for work.

Risk Management

The concept of risk management (involving in simple terms, the identification, assessment and elimination of risks to health and safety, or minimization if elimination is not reasonably practicable) is at the core of the WHS legislation in each state and territory. Each employer and person conducting a business or undertaking has broad obligations to implement a comprehensive system to achieve proactive risk management.

Officers of a Corporation

If an individual breaches their duty under WHS law, the criminal liability for that breach will apply to the individual, not to the corporation. Individuals who are convicted of a breach of WHS laws may be exposed to significant financial penalties and in the most serious cases, imprisonment. Queensland, Victoria, the Australian Capital Territory, the Northern Territory and Western Australia have all enacted legislation which creates an offence of industrial manslaughter.

The nature of personal liability differs between jurisdictions. For the harmonized jurisdictions (i.e., all states and territories except Victoria), an officer of a person conducting a business or undertaking that has a duty or obligation under the respective WHS Act must exercise 'due diligence' to ensure that the person conducting the business or undertaking complies with that duty or obligation. A failure by an officer to exercise due diligence is an offence. In Victoria, an officer of a corporation may be personally liable if the corporation is prosecuted for an offence against the relevant WHS law, and the offence of the corporation may be attributable to the officer failing to take reasonable care.

13.3. Rights of Workers

Workers are entitled to work in a safe work environment and are protected by laws against victimization or adverse action if the worker raises safety concerns.

In each state and territory, a duty holder has an obligation to consult with its workers about WHS issues to enable the workers to contribute to decisions affecting their health, safety and welfare at work. The specific requirements concerning consultation differ across states and territories.

In general terms, consultation requires:

- the sharing of relevant information about work health, safety and welfare with workers;
- that workers be given the opportunity to express their views and to contribute in a timely fashion to the resolution of work health, safety and welfare issues at their place of work; and
- that the views of workers are valued and taken into account.

Consultation on WHS matters is typically required before any change that may affect WHS matters is implemented, for example:

- when risks to health and safety arising from work are assessed or when the assessment of those risks is reviewed;
- when decisions are made about the measures to be taken to eliminate or control those risks;
- when introducing or altering the procedures for monitoring those risks (including health surveillance procedures);

- when decisions are made about the adequacy of facilities for the welfare of workers;
- when changes that may affect health, safety or welfare are proposed to the premises where persons work, to the systems or methods of work or to the plant or substances used for work; and
- when decisions are made about the procedures for consultation.

The FW Act regime defining the limited circumstances in which employees can take lawful industrial action (*see* section 9) does not apply if the action:

- was based on a reasonable concern of the employee about an imminent risk to his or her health and safety; and
- the employee did not unreasonably fail to comply with a direction of the employer to perform other available work, whether at the same or another workplace, that was safe and appropriate for the employee to perform.

The FW Act also contains particular protections from adverse action by employers against employees where that action is for reasons which include the workplace rights of that employee (*see* section 17).

Adverse action taken by an employer against an employee includes dismissing an employee, injuring the employee in his or her employment, altering the position of the employee to the employee's prejudice or discriminating between the employee and other employees. Some WHS issues will fall within the scope of the workplace rights which are protected under the adverse action provisions of the FW Act, for example:

- status as a safety representative within the workplace; or
- the employee's participation in proceedings in relation to a WHS prosecution.

13.4. Rights of Employers

An employer may direct a worker to follow safety requirements. Generally speaking, the failure of a worker to follow safety requirements can lead to disciplinary action, including termination of employment in more serious circumstances.

13.5. Injury or Accident at Work

All Australian jurisdictions have a no-fault scheme of workers' compensation that provides protection to workers and their employers in the event of a work-related injury or disease (*see* section 12 of this Chapter).

13.6. Workplace Violence

The risk of workplace violence must be managed in accordance with the general obligations of the duty holder under WHS laws. There have been a number of prosecutions which have resulted from failing to properly manage the risk of workplace violence, particularly in the areas of police or correction officers or other front-line social service staff dealing with the public in a potentially violent environment. Properly managing this risk may involve behavioural measures, such as 'buddy' arrangements and proper conflict resolution processes, as well as physical protections, such as workplace camera surveillance and security barriers.

13.7. Fines and Penalties

WHS laws are enforced through criminal convictions and a range of fines and penalties. The nature and severity of these fines and penalties vary between jurisdictions:

- Fines: Substantial fines can be imposed on individuals, officers, persons conducting a business or undertaking and bodies corporate. For example, in New South Wales, a body corporate may be fined up to AUD 3,721,686.00 for a reckless offence causing death or serious injury, and an officer or an individual person conducting a business or undertaking may be fined AUD 372,383.00 and AUD 744,229.00 respectively and/or imprisoned for five years. Further, in Queensland, for industrial manslaughter offences, a body corporate or an individual person conducting a business or undertaking may be fined up to AUD 10 million, and a senior officer may be imprisoned for twenty years. Depending on the jurisdiction, the severity of the fine will vary as a result of whether the duty holder's conduct was 'reckless', factors such as the company's history of offending, and the severity of the risk associated with a particular breach.
- Imprisonment: WHS offences are criminal matters, and the maximum penalty for an individual includes a term of imprisonment. It is however very rare for prosecuting authorities to pursue a custodial sentence.
- Other measures: There are a range of other measures which are typically used for more minor breaches, and it is not uncommon for inspectors and other WHS regulators to focus on remedial efforts rather than prosecution for a first offence, particularly if the offence does not result in an injury. Measures which the WHS regulator may consider include publicity orders, rectification orders and other remedial notices. For example, the relevant WHS authority may issue an Improvement Notice containing

directions to correct matters which appear, in the opinion of an inspector, to present an unacceptable risk and require certain measures to be taken.

13.8. Checklists of Dos and Don'ts

- Be aware of obligations under WHS law and the strict liability offences which are contained in that legislation. Be aware of the high standards which apply to duty-holder conduct. Information is available from state-based regulators, for example, SafeWork NSW, Workplace Health and Safety Queensland and WorkSafe Victoria.
- Provide information, instruction and training relevant to workers' duties and responsibilities in the workplace, including safety instruction, as required by the state WHS law.
- Develop robust safety systems and procedures, which ensure both formal compliance with regulatory standards and the development of a positive safety culture.
- Ensure management practices demonstrate all due diligence in relation to safety matters, including appropriate risk assessment, audit and follow-up of known risks.
- Make sure policies and procedures are communicated to workers.

Following an incident, an employer and relevant persons conducting a business or undertaking should:

- Notify the appropriate regulatory authority, for example, SafeWork NSW if the incident is of a type that is required to be notified under WHS law.
- Notify its insurance company.
- Provide a worker with a workers' compensation claim form if asked.
- Provide the injured worker with its workers' compensation insurance details in the event of an incident.
- Ensure that injured workers complete the register of injuries.

14. IMMIGRATION, SECONDMENT AND FOREIGN ASSIGNMENT

14.1. Overview

There are several options available to Australian employers who wish to sponsor overseas workers to work in Australia. However, as immigration is a highly regulated area in Australia, the legislation is frequently amended and substantial penalties can be imposed for contravention of the legislation. For this reason, it is recommended that employers seek the assistance of a registered immigration agent to assist with all enquiries in relation to immigration.

14.2. Secondment/Foreign Assignment

All workers lawfully working in Australia (other than on a temporary assignment) will be covered by Australian employment laws.

Depending on the nature and duration of the assignment, Australian employment laws will continue to govern Australian employees who are temporarily working outside of Australia.

14.3. Checklist of Dos and Don'ts

- Engage a registered migration agent for all enquiries in relation to the engagement of foreign workers in Australia.
- Carefully consider the nature and duration of Australian employees working on an assignment outside of Australia to determine whether new contractual arrangements need to be entered into.

15. RESTRICTIVE COVENANTS AND PROTECTION OF TRADE SECRETS AND CONFIDENTIAL INFORMATION

15.1. Overview

The employment relationship involves a range of implied duties between employees and employers. While the employment relationship continues, these duties include a duty of fidelity which broadly requires the employee to act consistently with the commercial interests of their employer. However, after the employment relationship comes to an end, an employer will generally need to rely on specific contractual protections to safeguard its commercial interests. Trade secrets can be regarded as a type of valuable confidential information of an employer.

Confidential Information

Information which is valuable to an employer may be protected by express covenants or by the equitable doctrine of breach of confidence. This doctrine applies to information that is supplied by one party to another and can arise independently of, and prior to, any contract of employment.

Generally speaking, confidential information is any information of a commercial nature which has been kept relatively secret. At common law, employees are subject to an implied duty of confidentiality. The problem for employers in relying on this implied duty or the equitable doctrine is the uncertainty as to what information a court will regard as confidential. Therefore, rather than rely on the implied duty or the equitable doctrine, it is preferable for an employer to obtain an express contractual promise which identifies and protects the relevant confidential information. Regardless of whether the implied duty or contractual obligation is relied upon, the information must truly be confidential in nature before it can be protected by law.

Factors which will assist an employer in proving that particular information is confidential include:

- only a limited number of people know the information;
- the information is stated to be confidential and is provided in circumstances which denote an obligation of confidence;
- steps are taken to ensure that the information remains secret;
- it would be difficult for others to obtain such information; and
- unauthorized use or disclosure of the information will cause the employer to suffer a detriment.

It is therefore incumbent upon employers who wish to establish that particular information is confidential to ensure that as many of these criteria as possible are met.

When drafting contractual restrictions on confidentiality, it is important to:

- identify the type of information the employer wishes to protect as clearly as possible (e.g., refer to a specific customer database or business strategy documents);
- include other obligations which may assist with the protection of confidential information (e.g., requiring property and computer equipment to be returned upon termination, or requiring the destruction of documents or other records); and
- impose practical measures to limit the circulation of documents or records, or require approval from an identified person to use certain information so as to help to remove doubt as to the confidentiality of the information.

Where an employer wishes to enforce the equitable doctrine of breach of confidence or the implied contractual duty of confidentiality, the employer must:

- be able to precisely identify the information in question;
- show that the information is confidential;
- show that the information was received by the employee from the employer in such circumstances as to import an obligation of confidence; and

– show that the employee is actually misusing, or threatening to misuse, the information without the employer's consent.

The equitable 'springboard principle' may also have application. This prevents a person who has obtained information in confidence to use that information to the detriment of the party who provided the information, even where the information has since become public. For example, this may prevent an ex-employee from using his or her knowledge in relation to the strategy, production and design of a forthcoming product to use that information to the detriment of their previous employer, even after the termination of his or her employment and after the detail has become more widely known.

15.2. Restrictive Covenants and Non-compete Agreements

Restraints of trade are typically implemented by a provision in the employment contract, providing that for a defined period of time following the termination of employment, the employee will not engage in various activities. These activities often include:

– working for competitor businesses;
– carrying out similar or competing work;
– soliciting current employees of the business to go and work for the new business;
– soliciting customers or clients of the business.

Ordinarily, an ex-employee may freely use information and know-how they have obtained during the course of their employment, provided they have not made deliberate attempts to acquire or memorize the information.

Further, the common law has long recognized that, as a matter of public policy, individuals should be free to take up employment with whomever they wish. Restraints of trade breach this fundamental public policy objective. For this reason, the courts regard restraints of trade as prima facie invalid. The burden, therefore, rests on a party seeking to enforce a restraint of trade to establish why it should be upheld and enforced by the court.

Under the Australian common law, the requirements for a restraint to be considered reasonable are:

(a) it must offer no more than adequate protection of the parties' legitimate interest favoured by the restraint (the employer) and has the burden of proving that the restraint is reasonable;
(b) the effect of the restraint on the position of the person restrained must be considered, ensuring that the individual enjoys the maximum freedom consistent with the protection necessary for the party who benefits from the restrictions;

(c) the restraint must be shown not to be contrary to the public interest. The onus of proof to show that it is contrary to the public interest rests on the party attacking the restraint; and
(d) the reasonableness of the restraint will be assessed, if it is made pursuant to a contract, in relation to the time at which the contract was entered into.

If the restraint does more than offer adequate protection of the legitimate interests, then it is likely to be considered invalid. The reasonableness of the restraint will include consideration of factors such as:

- subject matter – what conduct is being restrained?
- geography – what is the territorial scope of the restraint, and does it reflect the employer's commercial interests?
- duration – is the length of the restraint excessive?

For example, an employer seeks to restrain a business development executive from soliciting the employer's clients for a defined period following the termination of the employment. It may be considered legitimate to stop the business executive from soliciting business from those clients with whom he/she had direct dealings while employed. However, it would probably not be considered legitimate if the restraint sought to restrict him/her from contacting any client who did business with his/her employer, regardless of whether or not he/she had communications or contact with those clients.

Similarly, it may be considered legitimate to restrain the executive from contacting those clients for a limited period of time, for example, three months from the date of termination. It may not be considered legitimate to seek to prevent the executive from contacting them for two years from the date of termination, as this goes further than necessary to offer adequate protection.

To determine the effect of the restraint on the employee, the type of work the individual does and the marketplace in which they operate must be carefully considered. If the effect of the restraint is to basically make the individual unemployable or only able to secure employment at a much lower level to that seniority which they had achieved, it is more likely to be considered unreasonable.

Restraints of Trade Act 1976 (NSW)

In NSW, the common law position set out above has been modified by statute.

Section 4(1) of the *Restraints of Trade Act 1976* (NSW) (RTA) allows the court to 'read down' or enforce a restraint in a more limited form if the restraint appears to go beyond what is reasonable. The RTA does not, however, permit the court to rewrite the restraint provision. It cannot create a valid restraint out of an invalid one unless that can be done by narrowing the scope of the existing term. Section 4(3) of the RTA allows the court to order that a restraint provision is altogether invalid where there has been a manifest failure on the part of the person who drafted the restraint to make a reasonable restraint. Because of the application of the RTA, restraints are somewhat more likely to be upheld in NSW courts than in other Australian jurisdictions; however, it is still necessary to draft a provision with a view to the legitimate business interests it seeks to protect.

Remedies

Concerns in relation to confidential information or breaches of restrictive covenants are often urgent and immediate. With confidential information in particular, if a legal remedy is not quickly obtained, the opportunity to control the information may be lost altogether. An employer will often seek an interlocutory injunction, preventing the employee from acting on the information, contacting identified customers or commencing employment with a rival. To obtain an interlocutory injunction, the employer needs to show:

- a serious question to be tried (i.e., a sufficient likelihood of success to warrant the status quo being maintained while waiting for a hearing);
- that damages will not be a sufficient remedy; and
- that the balance of convenience favours granting the order.

15.3. Checklist of Dos and Don'ts

- Ensure restrictive covenants are drafted in light of the specific circumstances and reflect the legitimate commercial interests the employer wishes to protect.
- Do not rely on a generic clause for all employees – consider the employee's specific skills, customer connections, seniority and access to information.
- Ensure that information you wish to protect as confidential information is properly safeguarded during the course of employment.

16. PROTECTION OF WHISTLE-BLOWING CLAIMS

16.1. Overview

On 1 July 2019, the Australian Federal Parliament passed the Treasury Laws Amendment (Enhancing Whistleblower Protections) Act 2019 (*Whistleblower Protection Act*).

The Whistleblower Protection Act essentially:

- harmonizes the various current whistle-blower regimes under federal law;
- extends obligations to all public and large proprietary companies;

- provides a wider scope of corporate misconduct that can be the subject of a protected disclosure, including the existence of an 'improper state of affairs';
- widens the range of people who can qualify for whistle-blower protection;
- expands the existing protections and remedies for whistle-blowers;
- allows anonymous disclosures.

However, the Whistleblower Protection Act excludes most disclosures of personal work-related grievances from protection.

The Whistleblower Protection Act requires public companies and 'large proprietary companies' to have mandatory whistle-blower policies. The whistle-blower policy must include details in relation to:

- the protections available to whistle-blowers;
- the person or organization to whom protected disclosures may be made;
- how the company will support whistle-blowers and protect them from detriment;
- how the company will investigate protected disclosures.

Failure to comply with the requirement to have a whistle-blower policy will expose the company to a penalty of AUD 165,000.00.

In limited circumstances, if an employee complains to their employer about matters arising in the course of employment or in relation to WHS, that employee may have certain protections afforded by specific state legislation.

Legislation in the Public Sector

Whistle-blower legislation has existed in the public sector since the early 1990s. Most states and territories have some form of legislation.

Broadly, legislation dealing with whistle-blowing seeks to provide protection to persons who disclose corrupt, improper or unlawful conduct in the public sector (e.g., mismanagement or maladministration of public resources or risk to public health and safety or the environment).

Legislation in each state differs, particularly in relation to who may make a protected disclosure as well as the criteria necessary for the disclosure to be protected. However, most of the legislation imposes obligations on state government agencies to investigate a disclosure. Further, state government agencies must take steps to protect those who make protected disclosures. It is an offence for someone to take detrimental action against, or to victimize, a person who has made a protected disclosure.

Victimization in Respect of Complaints

In some circumstances, it is unlawful to victimize an employee as a result of their making a complaint or participation in a complaint process in the context of employment. *See* sections 13 and 17.

16.2. Checklist of Dos and Don'ts

(1) Understand whether the whistle-blowing provisions in the Whistleblower Protection Act apply to a particular company, or whether legislation governing public sector organizations applies.
(2) Ensure that a policy is in place which sets out guidelines with respect to whistle-blowing by employees or other persons. The policy should set out a clear framework for the manner in which whistle-blowing will be handled by the organization.
(3) Conduct training for relevant employees in the company to ensure there is a clear understanding of the whistle-blowing provisions including:
  (a) the roles and responsibilities of various employees in the company;
  (b) the confidentiality obligations of persons who receive information which would be subject to protection;
  (c) the obligations of the reporting employee and the organization once a whistle-blowing claim is made; and
  (d) the prohibition of victimization or reprisal towards a person connected with the making of a whistle-blowing allegation.

17. PROHIBITION OF DISCRIMINATION IN THE WORKPLACE

17.1. Overview of Anti-discrimination Laws

Australia has both federal and state anti-discrimination laws that are designed to promote, among other things, equality of opportunity in the workplace. Although the grounds for discrimination vary from jurisdiction to jurisdiction, generally, the law prevents both direct and indirect discrimination on the basis of certain proscribed attributes, such as age, breastfeeding, gender identity, physical or intellectual impairment, industrial activity, employment activity, lawful sexual activity, marital status, parental/carer's status, family responsibilities, physical features, political belief or activity, pregnancy, race, religious belief or activity, sex, sexual orientation and personal association with a person who is identified by reference to any of these attributes.

Direct discrimination occurs when an employer treats, or proposes to treat, a person with a proscribed attribute less favourably than they would treat someone without that attribute in the same or similar circumstances.

Indirect discrimination occurs when an employer imposes a requirement, condition or practice that is intended to be fair but has the effect of discriminating against a person (or group of persons) with a proscribed attribute. Where the outcome of a requirement, condition or practice is that a higher proportion of people without the attribute can comply, and where the requirement is not considered to be reasonable in all the circumstances, then it may be in breach of anti-discrimination legislation.

In the pre-employment context, an employer must not discriminate against prospective employees in determining who should be offered employment, either in the terms on which employment is offered, by refusing or deliberately omitting to offer employment, or by denying a future employee's access to occupational training or retraining.

In respect of existing employees, where an employer denies or limits access to opportunities for promotion, transfer, training or any other benefits, dismisses an employee or otherwise terminates their employment, denies the employee's access to occupational training or retraining or subjects an employee to any other detriment on the basis of an attribute, this may result in unlawful discrimination.

These legislative prohibitions extend to the relationship between principal and independent contractor.

A proscribed attribute or attributes need not be the sole or dominant cause of discriminatory conduct. An employee is only required to prove, on the balance of probabilities, that an attribute was a reason for the differential treatment. The motive of the person engaging in discriminatory behaviour is irrelevant.

An employer may be vicariously liable for the acts of their employees in the workplace or away from the workplace where the offending conduct has a sufficient nexus with an employee's employment. For example, when the employee is attending a work-related conference or a party organized by the employer.

In order to defend a vicarious liability claim, employers need to demonstrate that they have taken reasonable precautions to prevent or minimize the occurrence of discriminatory conduct in the workplace. Importantly, employers must ensure that they have implemented diversity/equal opportunity policies in the workplace, that all employees and contractors have received adequate training in respect of those policies and accompanying procedures and that steps have been taken to ensure that those policies and procedures are adhered to at all levels within the employer's organization.

Exceptions and Exemptions

There are a number of exceptions and exemptions to discrimination in the employment context, including where the genuine occupational requirements of the position necessitate discrimination on the basis of age, sex, race, impairment or physical feature, or where the acts are reasonably necessary to protect health and safety. A number of specific exceptions and exemptions are discussed in further detail below.

Remedies

While remedies differ across jurisdictions, broadly speaking, a tribunal or court may grant an injunction requiring a person to refrain from discriminatory conduct; impose a penalty; order payment of compensation for damages or injury incurred, including loss of wages; and/or make any order to redress resulting loss, including the issuance of an apology, reinstatement or backdating a promotion or entitlement.

Employers may, following an investigation into any allegations of discrimination, and upon being satisfied that the employee has more likely than not engaged in discrimination, lawfully discipline an employee or terminate an employee's employment for a serious breach of policy and/or the terms of the employment contract.

17.2. Age Discrimination

Generally, employers cannot refuse to employ a person or cannot provide benefits based on a person's age. However, there are a number of exceptions to this requirement. For example, compulsory retirement for judicial officers is not unlawful discrimination, and neither is compulsory retirement for public sector employees where the Minister has granted an exemption. However, compulsory retirement is prohibited for other types of employees in most Australian jurisdictions. In certain circumstances, reduced wages for those under the age of 21 do not constitute unlawful discrimination.

17.3. Race Discrimination

Racial discrimination generally involves discrimination based on colour, nationality or ethnic origin, including custom and language. Racial discrimination prohibits discrimination against all individuals, regardless of whether they are members of minority or majority groups.

Federal and state laws also protect against racial vilification and racial harassment. This involves expressions of intolerance of a particular race or inciting hatred, contempt or ridicule of a race. For example, claims that all Pakistanis are terrorists are prohibited.

17.4. SEX DISCRIMINATION/SEXUAL HARASSMENT

Sex discrimination is discrimination based on whether a person is male, female or transgender (including those who assume the bodily characteristics of the opposite sex or seek to live as, or identify as, a member of the opposite sex).

Where the genuine operational requirements of a role require a person of a particular sex (e.g., models for women's/men's clothing or security guards required to physically examine persons), exclusion of employees of a particular sex will not constitute unlawful discrimination.

To avoid indirect discrimination, any condition imposed by an employer must be reasonable in the relevant circumstances. For example, where it would amount to 'unjustifiable hardship' to provide separate toilets for females in the workplace, the condition to use unisex toilets will not amount to unlawful discrimination.

Pursuant to the FW Act, FWC may also make an equal remuneration order on application by an employee, employee organization or the Sex Discrimination Commissioner. These orders require that remuneration for male and female workers is equal, where work of equal or comparable value is performed.

The Sex Discrimination Commissioner forms part of the Australian Human Rights Commission (together with the Aboriginal and Torres Strait Islander Social Justice Commissioner, Disability Discrimination Commissioner, Human Rights Commissioner, Race Discrimination Commissioner and the Commissioner responsible for Age Discrimination). The Commissioners have responsibility for administering the relevant federal anti-discrimination and human rights laws, including investigating and conciliating complaints, developing education programmes and providing legal advice and submissions to courts and the government in relation to the observance of human rights.

17.5. HANDICAP AND DISABILITY DISCRIMINATION

Discrimination on the basis of impairment includes any physical or mental disability or physical features. Physical features include naturally occurring features such as weight, height, size or disfigurement, but may also relate to voluntarily acquired features, including tattoos or body piercings.

An employer may lawfully discriminate against an employee on the basis of an impairment in circumstances where genuine occupational requirements necessitate particular capabilities. However, an employer must ensure that they do not make unjustified assumptions about a person's abilities (always act on medical or other expert advice) and must also consider whether any special services or facilities may 'reasonably' be implemented to allow that employee to perform their role. There is no definition of what is 'reasonable'. However, the employer should consider the cost, the effect on the employer, any impact on productivity, whether the special services or facilities will in fact assist the employee in performing their role and the impact on the employee of not providing the special services or facilities.

For example, an employer may be required to supply a raised desk or alter a workspace to accommodate an employee with back problems or use symbols instead of colours to assist colour-blind employees to safely and adequately perform their job. This may include ensuring reasonable access for employees with disabilities.

17.6. National Extraction or Social Origin Discrimination

Federal law protects against discrimination in employment on the basis of national extraction or social origin. National extraction refers to the nationality of a person, the country in which the person was born or their citizenship. Social origin refers to a person's status or class within society.

For example, a refusal to offer a person employment because they are Asian or come from a particular town or suburb, or perhaps went to a particular school, would be prohibited conduct.

17.7. Religious Discrimination

Religious-based discrimination may occur in relation to identification with a particular religion or ethnoreligious origin, for example, Judaism, or alternatively, refraining from identifying with any religion.

The most common form of unlawful discrimination in this area is discrimination in the application of a dress code. Although an employer may set a dress standard, where the standard offends religious beliefs and is otherwise unreasonable, it will amount to unlawful discrimination. Therefore, in most cases where an employee wishes to wear a headscarf or turban with their uniform, the employer will act unlawfully if it refuses such requests.

There are specific exemptions in respect of discrimination in religious institutions and schools. Provided that discrimination is required in order to comply with genuine religious beliefs or principles, it will not be unlawful discrimination. For example, where a teacher at a Catholic school openly expresses beliefs contrary to Catholicism, their employment may be lawfully terminated to protect the potential vulnerability of students with respect to their faith.

17.8. Military Status Discrimination

Military status is not a ground for unlawful discrimination in Australia.

17.9. Pregnancy Discrimination

It is unlawful to discriminate against a person in respect of employment because they are pregnant or intend to fall pregnant. Employers should not refuse employment, training or promotional opportunities because of pregnancy or potential pregnancy. Employers should therefore be cautious when asking an employee whether they are or intend to become pregnant.

Discrimination on the Basis of Parental/Carer's Status and Breastfeeding is also unlawful under federal and most state anti-discrimination legislation.

In order to avoid unlawful discrimination, an employer will need to take reasonable steps to accommodate parental or caregiver responsibilities. For example, this could include (where it is reasonable) the offering of part-time employment or flexible hours or rescheduling meetings to the working days of part-time staff.

Where it is not reasonable for the employer to accommodate parental responsibilities, for example, where the employee cannot adequately perform their work from home, insistence on the standard working arrangements will not result in unlawful discrimination. However, the employer should consider all options which may allow the employee to fulfil the relevant requirements of their position and any refusal should be based upon reasonable grounds.

Although each request should be considered on a case-by-case basis, employers should consult their jurisdictional requirements to ensure compliance with legislative processes for considering requests for flexible working arrangements. For example, under the FW Act, employers are required to approve or refuse a request for flexible working arrangements within twenty-one working days of the request being made. A bare refusal is insufficient and details of the refusal must be given in writing. The refusal has to be based on 'reasonable business grounds'. 'Reasonable business grounds' is not defined in the legislation. However, factors to consider include the effect on the workplace, the ability to reorganize work among staff, the cost to the employer, any impact on productivity and customer service and any implications of refusal for the employee.

In accordance with the FW Act, an employer may require a pregnant female employee to take parental leave or transfer to a different position temporarily where their pregnancy does not allow them to safely perform their current role. Any such decision should be based on medical evidence. In circumstances where the employer reallocates work in order to protect a pregnant employee and it was safe for them to perform their ordinary role, this will result in discrimination.

17.10. Marital Status Discrimination

It is unlawful to discriminate against a person in employment on the basis of their marital status. Discrimination on the basis of marital status includes the selection of (or failure to select) an employee for employment or benefits in connection with their employment based upon their marital status.

For example, an employer cannot select employees for redundancy on the basis of their marital status.

17.11. Sexual Orientation Discrimination

Discrimination on the basis of sexuality, sexual preference, homosexuality, transsexuality, transgender and lawful sexual activity are prohibited grounds of discrimination in employment. However, the precise grounds vary between jurisdictions.

Generally speaking, sexuality encompasses a person's sexual orientation, including homosexuality and bisexuality. Transsexuality refers to people who have assumed the bodily characteristics of the opposite sex. Transgender has an even wider definition and refers to people who identify as a member of the opposite sex and people of indeterminate sex who identify with a particular sex. Lawful sexual activity excludes any criminal conduct such as paedophilia.

An employer must not fail to offer a potential employee employment, terminate an employee's employment or offer or fail to offer employees benefits in connection with an employee's employment on the basis of their sexuality or sexual preference or because they engage in a lawful sexual relationship with a particular person.

17.12. Retaliation/Victimization

Victimization occurs when a person subjects or threatens to subject another person to a detriment because that person has made a complaint or allegation against another person, has brought a proceeding in relation to discrimination or sexual harassment or has been involved in the giving of information or evidence in relation to a complaint. Victimization is prohibited by both state and federal anti-discrimination legislation.

An employer must not subject an employee to detriment on the basis that they have made a complaint against the employer or have been involved in the resolution of a complaint (e.g., as a witness or support person). For example, an employer must not engage in performance management of an employee or demote the employee because they have made a complaint or given information in respect of a complaint.

17.13. Fair Work Legislation

The FW Act's general protection provisions (*see* section 11) prohibit an employer from taking certain adverse actions against an employee or prospective employee on the basis of race, colour, sex, sexual preference, age, physical or mental disability, marital status, family or carer's responsibilities, pregnancy, religion, political opinion, national extraction or social origin. They also make it unlawful to terminate an employee's employment while they are temporarily absent from work (less than three months, although referred to the Fair Work Regulations with respect to the exceptions) due to illness or injury.

Further, an employer is prohibited from coercing or exerting undue influence or pressure on an employee to exercise or not exercise a workplace right or to engage or not engage in industrial activity. 'Industrial activity' includes joining an industrial association, engaging in or promoting lawful industrial activity or advancing the views of an industrial association.

These prohibitions also apply in respect of the principal/independent contractor relationship.

An employer will not be in breach of the FW Act general protection provisions where the action taken is not unlawful under any anti-discrimination law in force in the place, where the action is taken because of the inherent requirements of the position or where the action is taken in good faith, by a religious institution, in order to avoid injury to religious susceptibilities of adherents of that religion or creed.

Breach of any of these provisions of the FW Act may result in a penalty of up to AUD 82,500 for a body corporate.

17.14. Bullying and Harassment

Since January 2014, bullying is expressly prohibited by legislation. A worker who reasonably believes that he or she has been bullied at work may apply to the FWC for an order to stop bullying. It should be noted that in these circumstances, the FWC only has the power to grant an order to stop the bullying – it cannot award compensation.

In addition, it is generally accepted that bullying may amount to a breach of relevant WHS laws, anti-discrimination laws (where the bullying includes actions based on proscribed attributes) and potentially criminal law.

The model WHS laws (*see* section 13) impose a general duty on persons conducting a business or undertaking to, so far as is reasonably practicable, ensure the health and safety of their workers and other persons who may be affected by work carried out as part of the conduct of the business or undertaking.

Bullying occurs when an individual or group of individuals repeatedly behave unreasonably towards a worker or a group of workers that creates a risk to health and safety. It can be direct (obvious) or indirect (subtle) and includes behaviour such as verbal or physical abuse, spreading misinformation or malicious rumours, interfering with personal property or work equipment, deliberately excluding someone from normal work activities, setting tasks that are unreasonable and deliberately denying access to information and resources.

Additionally, in Victoria, the scope of behaviours that may form the basis of the crime of stalking was extended in 2011. Making threats, directing abusive or offensive words or acts to the victim, and acting in any other way that could reasonably be expected to cause physical or mental harm to the victim (including psychological harm, suicidal thoughts and self-harm) or arouses apprehension or fear in the victim for their own safety or the safety of others, now fall within the definition of stalking under the Victorian *Crimes Act 1958*. While not specifically directed at employers or employees, the provisions are capable of applying in the workplace context. Persons found guilty of stalking can face up to ten years in jail, and victims of these types of workplace bullying can apply for intervention orders even where the bully has not been found guilty of a crime.

In order to comply with their health and safety duties, employers should implement and provide adequate training on workplace policies and procedures to ensure that all employees are aware of the types of conduct that constitute bullying and harassment, that such conduct is prohibited and that all complaints be taken seriously and be appropriately investigated and resolved. To avoid or reduce the likelihood of allegations of bullying being made, employers should assist supervisors in managing their employees' workload and check that workload, delegation of tasks and assessment of performance are reasonable.

17.15. Sexual Harassment

Sexual harassment occurs when a person makes unwelcome sexual advances, a request for sexual favours or engages in unwelcome conduct of a sexual nature, in circumstances in which a 'reasonable person', having regard to the circumstances, would have anticipated that another person would be offended, humiliated or intimidated. The intention of the perpetrator is irrelevant. Sexual harassment includes foul language, intrusive questions, unwanted sexual advances, displaying or viewing of pornographic materials, dirty jokes, insults or taunts.

State and federal laws prohibit sexual harassment. It is clear that employers may be held vicariously liable for sexual harassment by their employees or agents, where that conduct occurs within the workplace. It is also possible for employers to be held vicariously liable for sexual harassment by their employees or agents where that conduct occurs outside of the workplace, provided that there is a sufficient nexus or close connection between the sexual harassment and the employment (cases involving sexual harassment outside of the workplace include harassment at parties organized by an employer, at work-related conferences attended by employees and in circumstances where accommodations are organized by an employer).

In order to defend a claim of vicarious liability, an employer must demonstrate that they have taken reasonable precautions to prevent or minimize the occurrence of sexual harassment. This may include the implementation of policies and procedures for preventing and investigating claims of sexual harassment.

It is important to ensure that employees respect each other's sensitivities and avoid making sexually suggestive remarks, jokes or behaviours in the workplace.

Further, it is important that any incidents of sexual harassment are promptly investigated and resolved and that the employer takes all reasonable steps to prevent the occurrence of further incidents. Engaging in sexual harassment may constitute grounds for dismissal, particularly where the employer can demonstrate that the employee was aware of and attended training in respect of the company's workplace policy prohibiting sexual harassment.

On 5 January 2020, the Sex Discrimination Commissioner of the Australian Human Rights Commission released the 'Respect@Work: Sexual Harassment National Inquiry Report'(Report) calling for a new regulatory model to contend with sexual harassment in the workplace that improves the coordination, consistency and clarity between the anti-discrimination, employment and WHS legislative schemes.

On 8 April 2021, the Australian Government released 'A Roadmap for Respect: Preventing and Addressing Sexual Harassment in Australian Workplaces' (Roadmap for Respect) which responds to all fifty-five of the Australian Human Rights Commission's recommendations in the Respect@Work Report. The Roadmap for Respect notes whether they are matters for the States or the private sector to address and implement and outlines the path forward for Australia to prevent and address sexual harassment and to support cultural change in the workplace. The Roadmap for Respect is designed to complement the existing work under the current 'National Plan to Reduce Violence Against Women and their Children (2010–2022)' and to ensure alignment with the development of the next National Plan.

On 12 December 2022, the *Anti-Discrimination and Human Rights Legislation Amendment (Respect at Work) Act 2022* (Cth) commenced. This legislation implements various changes recommended by the Report and most significantly, creates a positive duty for employers or a person conducting a business or undertaking to take reasonable and proportionate measures to eliminate, as far as possible, sex discrimination, sexual harassment, victimization, and conduct that is unlawful under the new provisions relating to 'hostile workplace environments'.[5] The positive duty commences on 13 December 2023.

17.16. Constructive Discharge/Constructive Dismissal

When an employer discriminates against an employee such that the employee has no choice but to leave their employment, this may, in addition to being a breach of anti-discrimination legislation, result in a constructive dismissal (*see* section 5 for further detail regarding unfair dismissal and unlawful termination).

Constructive dismissal may occur, for example, where an employee cannot meet the requirement of an employer to attend early morning planning meetings due to parental responsibilities and cannot practically continue in their role without attending such meetings (where such a requirement is not reasonable). It may also occur when an employee cannot continue in their role due to ongoing discrimination or harassment having an adverse effect on their health.

17.17. Checklist of Dos and Don'ts

- Do not ask inappropriate questions in an interview, as these may lead to a conclusion that the employer did or did not employ the person because of a particular attribute or discriminated in the terms and conditions upon which employment was offered.

5. A work environment will be 'hostile' if it is offensive, intimidating or humiliating [to a person] by reason of two or more matters that include the sex or characteristic of the person, whether or not the sex or the characteristic is the dominant or substantial reason. Whether or not conduct is offensive, intimidating or humiliating is judged from the perspective of a reasonable person.

- Do not make assumptions about a person's abilities. Only impose genuine and reasonable requirements and conditions in employment following objective consideration of medical or other expert advice. Always consider whether these conditions may be met by implementing special services or facilities or flexible work arrangements.
- Accurately document any decision to transfer, promote or in any way change the terms and conditions of employment. Ensure that genuine, non-discriminatory reasons apply to each decision.
- Where possible, provide equal access to promotional and training opportunities for all employees. Training and promotional opportunities must be based on merit and skill.
- Implement training, policies and procedures to inform employees of what is acceptable workplace behaviour and to prevent discrimination, bullying and harassment. Actively enforce these policies and procedures in accordance with their terms.
- Investigate all complaints regarding discrimination, bullying and harassment seriously and in a timely manner.
- Ensure that employees who have breached company policies or procedures are dealt with appropriately, either by taking lawful disciplinary action or dismissing the employee where serious misconduct occurs.
- Accurately document any investigation or disciplinary process.

18. SMOKING IN THE WORKPLACE

18.1. Overview

Smoke-free policies now exist in the vast majority of Australian workplaces, including all Commonwealth and state government departments and most private companies. In particular:

- in NSW, the *Smoke-Free Environment Act 2000* (NSW) prohibits smoking in enclosed public places and certain outdoor public areas;
- in Victoria, the *Tobacco Act 1987* (Vic) prohibits smoking in enclosed workplaces and many public places;
- in Queensland, the *Tobacco and Other Smoking Products Act 1998* (Qld) prohibits smoking in enclosed places and many outdoor areas;
- in the ACT, the *Smoke-Free Public Places Act 2003* (ACT) prohibits smoking in enclosed public areas and other outdoor areas;
- in South Australia, the *Tobacco Products Regulation Act 1997* (SA) prohibits smoking in enclosed workplaces and enclosed public dining, cafes, lifts, public entertainment venues and some outdoor areas;

- in Tasmania, the *Public Health Act 1997* (Tas) prohibits smoking in all enclosed public spaces and workplaces; and
- in Western Australia, the *Occupational Safety and Health Regulations 1996* (WA) prohibit smoking in enclosed workplaces and the *Tobacco Products Control Act 2006* (WA) prohibits smoking in public places.

The exception to the general rule of smoke-free workplaces only arises in certain 'public' workplaces, such as hotels, clubs, nightclubs, bars, restaurants and casinos (especially private gaming areas). The scope of these exemptions varies from state to state. For example, in 2007, the general exemption in NSW for hotels, clubs, nightclubs and casinos was removed. In each state where an exemption is available, there are commonly accompanying requirements in relation to matters such as ventilation, providing comparable smoke-free areas and the erection of barriers or partitions. In addition, there is a large body of industry or transport-specific legislation that deals with anti-smoking requirements, such as displaying appropriate signage.

Potential Liabilities for Employers

General industrial safety requirements, including employers' general obligations in relation to WHS, impose obligations and create liabilities with respect to smoking in the workplace. In 1994, the 'National Occupational Health and Safety Commission released Guidance Note on Passive Smoking in the Workplace' (NOHSC:3019 (1994)), which highlighted smoking as a WHS issue. Criminal penalties apply for breach of these obligations, including potential personal liability for company directors and managers (*see* section 13).

Civil Litigation

Companies that allow smoking in their workplace are at risk of being the subject of civil proceedings by either employees or members of the public who suffer health problems as a result of passive smoking. Such litigation is frequently focussed on forensic questions of causation in relation to injuries alleged to have been caused by passive exposure to tobacco smoke. Depending on the circumstances, applicants may seek compensation by reference to common law negligence claims or statutory workers' compensation entitlements.

Australia has been an active jurisdiction in tobacco-related litigation:

- In 1992, the NSW District Court decision in *Scholem v. NSW Department of Health* (27 May 1992) was the world's first jury verdict on an employer's negligence in regard to passive smoking. The case found the employer to be negligent, and in violation of WHS legislation in force at the time.

- In 2000, the Commonwealth Human Rights and Equal Opportunity Commission's decision in *Meeuwissen v. Hilton Hotels of Australia Pty Ltd* (Complaint H97/50 and H97/51; 25 September 1997 and 10 March 2000) became the first successful disability discrimination complaint in relation to no-smoking areas. The Commission upheld a complaint by patrons affected by asthma on the basis that the absence of a no-smoking area within a hotel constituted disability discrimination.

In each Australian state and territory, there is a specific statutory scheme which provides for compensation of workplace injuries on a no-fault basis (*see* section 11.4). An injury in this context will include a disease contracted in the course of employment (where the employment was a contributing factor) and the aggravation of a disease (where the employment was a contributing factor).

As noted above, under WHS laws, employers and persons conducting a business or undertaking have a duty to ensure the health and safety of workers and others at their place of work. There is a range of non-binding guidance material available to help employers comply with their WHS obligations. For example, the 'Smoke-Free Workplaces – A Guide for Workplaces in South Australia' was published by SA Health to assist workplaces in meeting their legal requirements and developing smoke-free policies.

Smoke-Free Policies and Termination of Employment

Where there is a smoke-free policy at a workplace, companies should ensure that employees who breach the policy are treated with procedural fairness.

For example, in *Bostic (Australia) Pty Limited v. Gorgevski* (No. 2) (1992) 36 FCR 439, the Full Bench of the Federal Court of Australia upheld a decision to award compensation to a long-standing employee who was summarily dismissed for smoking in a non-smoking area in breach of company policy. Although the company had circulated its smoke-free policy (in English), the employee was of Macedonian background and spoke poor English, and had not been made aware that the policy provided for instant dismissal where an employee breached the smoking prohibition.

18.2. Checklist of Dos and Don'ts

- Be aware that smoking is a workplace safety issue.
- Understand applicable state legislation prohibiting smoking and ensure workplace policies comply with those requirements.

– Ensure that workplace smoking policies are clearly communicated to employees and ensure they are implemented with procedural fairness in mind.

19. USE OF DRUGS AND ALCOHOL IN THE WORKPLACE

19.1. OVERVIEW: USE OF DRUGS AND ALCOHOL IN THE WORKPLACE

The use of drugs and alcohol in the workplace raises a number of industrial relations and WHS issues. Typically, the use of illegal drugs and the unauthorized consumption of alcohol use in the workplace would constitute grounds for disciplinary action, including the termination of employment. Consequently, there is often considerable industrial resistance to the introduction of drug and alcohol testing.

From a legal perspective, there needs to be a foundation for requiring employees or other persons to undertake drug and alcohol testing. Usually, testing may be permitted if an employee's contract of employment provides for testing, the employee consents to testing or it is reasonable under the circumstances for the employee to be tested. What is reasonable under the circumstances will depend, for example, on whether the work performed by the employee is in high-risk industries such as heavy industrialized and manufacturing sites, mining or construction. If an employee refuses to undergo testing, depending on the circumstances, disciplinary action may follow.

Increasingly, employers are introducing drug and alcohol policies relying upon their duties to ensure safe workplaces. These policies set out the employer's expectations in relation to the use and consumption of drugs and alcohol at work, including the disciplinary consequences if an employee is found to be under the influence of drugs and alcohol at work.

Policies of this nature are most common in high-risk industries where employees are operating machinery or equipment, or it is otherwise essential that they are not impaired by drugs or alcohol (e.g., in the transport industry). However, the method and frequency of drug and alcohol testing remains a contentious issue.

Method of Testing

The particular method of drug and alcohol testing, for example, saliva- or urine-based, involves balancing safety considerations against employee privacy concerns.

For example, in one case, it was found that an employer's proposed urine testing regime would be unjust and unreasonable and would not necessarily indicate that a worker was unfit for work. The employer had argued that urine testing, as opposed to saliva testing, was a better method for detecting drugs and alcohol in the human system, as urine testing is capable of detecting drugs ingested days before the test, whereas oral fluid testing is only capable of detecting drugs ingested hours before the test. However, on the evidence before it, the Australian Industrial Relations Commission (now FWC) was not satisfied that the benefit of urine testing outweighed the impact on a worker's privacy.

Frequency of Testing

Whether drug and alcohol testing in a workplace is to be systematic or random is also often a contentious issue.

In a recent ruling, FWC allowed the introduction of random drug and alcohol testing at a major oil refinery in New South Wales. In that case, FWC had to consider whether random testing should be included in the provisions of an industrial agreement. FWC considered that the employer had an absolute obligation under WHS laws to ensure safety on-site and that there was a large risk that an employee under the influence of drugs and alcohol could cause a devastating accident. They held that the introduction of the testing was justifiable, even balanced against the privacy concerns of the employees.

In some industries, there is specific legislation that regulates drug and alcohol testing. For example, in the rail industry, the *Rail Safety Act 2008* (*Act*) and the *Rail Safety (Drug and Alcohol Testing) Regulation 2008* (*Regulation*) provides the main regulatory framework. Under the Act, a rail transport operator must, as part of its safety management system, have a drug and alcohol management programme for rail safety workers who carry out, or are about to carry out, rail safety work in connection with railway operations for which the operator is required to be accredited.

Only rail safety workers who are carrying out, or are about to carry out, rail safety work are subject to testing under the Regulation. However, a rail transport operator may have a drug and alcohol policy which requires all of its employees to be tested, and most rail operators have such a policy.

General Employer Liability

The service of alcohol at any work-related or sponsored function can lead to antisocial behaviour by employees, which, in turn, leads to potential claims such as sexual harassment or discrimination claims. Employees may also bring workers' compensation claims against employers in circumstances where employees have injured themselves at work-sponsored functions after consuming drugs or alcohol.

It is important that employers outline to their staff prior to any work-sponsored event at which alcohol will be served according to the expectations of employees, including the consequences of antisocial behaviour. Employers should make reference to any applicable drug and alcohol or disciplinary policies in any such communication.

19.2. Checklist of Dos and Don'ts

- In the development and introduction of a drug and alcohol policy, consider the level of consultation with employees. Generally speaking, employee consultation will assist in the acceptance of the policy.
- Consider carefully what disciplinary process is to be used if an employee is under the influence of drugs or alcohol, or refuses to be tested. For example, will there be a staged disciplinary process by which an employee would receive a first warning? Or, in the circumstances of the employer's industry, would it warrant summary termination?
- Employers should also think carefully about the type of drug and alcohol testing (if any) that they propose to use in the workplace having regard to the legal basis upon which the employer may implement testing, and whether the frequency and type of proposed testing is suitable for the employer's particular workforce.
- Develop an employee assistance programme that involves appropriate counselling and support mechanisms for employees with drug and alcohol problems.
- Do not institute arbitrary and onerous drug and alcohol testing procedures which do not match the particular workforce's needs.

20. AIDS, HIV, SARS, BLOOD-BORNE PATHOGENS

20.1. Overview

In Australia, managing the risk of infection of HIV/AIDS, SARS and other blood-borne pathogens in the workplace arises predominantly in two employment law contexts: WHS and discrimination.

Work Health and Safety

WHS obligations are set out in section 13. The obligation to ensure the health, safety and welfare of workers gives rise to a duty to ensure that workers are not exposed to risks to their health, such as the possibility of HIV/AIDS, SARS or other blood-borne pathogens infection. For example, an employer has an obligation to ensure that all workers are not exposed to the risk of such blood-borne pathogen infections when they are at an employer's place of work.

Exposure to blood-borne viruses such as Hepatitis and HIV/AIDS within the workplace can be prevented if employers follow risk management processes. In particular, they have to identify the hazard (e.g., an HIV-infected person working with sharp machinery in close proximity to fellow workers), assess the risk and implement procedures to control the risk.

In an effort to address the issues arising out of these risks, a Code of Practice for the Control of Work-Related Exposure to Hepatitis and HIV (Blood-Borne) Viruses (the Code of Practice) has been approved by the NOHSC. The first edition of the Code of Practice was released in 1993, and it has been updated since that time. Many states have adopted the Code of Practice.

As stated in section 13, new WHS legislation commenced in some states on 1 January 2012. Transitional arrangements have been made such that existing jurisdictional codes remain in force until a replacement model Code of Practice is approved. The Code of Practice has not been replaced and therefore remains in force in all jurisdictions that adopted the Code of Practice. The Code of Practice requires that employers follow a two-stage hazard identification process. They have to:

- identify potential sources of infection; and
- identify activities and occupations where hazards exist, and there are potential means of transmission, for example, during the provision of first aid, or when cleaning toilets.

The Code of Practice identifies some examples of sources of infection, such as blood and bodily fluids, and likely activities or occupations where a hazard may exist, which include cleaning staff, first aid providers, security workers and sanitation workers. It then provides a range of factors that must be taken into account in the assessment of the risk arising from the hazards which include the type and frequency of exposure to blood or bodily fluids, or to contaminated materials and the volume and frequency of contact with discarded used needles and syringes. The Code of Practice also provides examples of controls that may be used. Some examples provided include safe work procedures, an infection control programme, training and supervision and personal protective equipment.

The Code of Practice also sets out guidelines for workers with Hepatitis B, Hepatitis C or HIV/AIDS. These guidelines set out general precautions to prevent transmission of the disease, including simple steps such as covering cuts and abrasions and general personal hygiene.

Ultimately, it is the employer and employee's responsibility to work together to identify and mitigate the risks arising in the workplace from those persons with these types of infectious diseases.

Discrimination

Employers also have obligations under federal and state discrimination legislation to ensure that they do not discriminate on the basis of disability or impairment.

The definitions of disability vary between state and federal legislation; however, generally, HIV/AIDS and infections such as Hepatitis C would fall within the definition of 'impairment' or 'disability'. For example, in Victoria, 'impairment' is defined as:

- the presence in the body of an organism that may cause disease;
- total or partial loss of a part of the body;
- malfunction or disfigurement of a part of the body.

Employers must not:

- discriminate against an employee because of the employee's infection (such as having Hepatitis C or HIV/AIDS), unless that person is unable to perform the inherent requirements of the role; or
- impose unreasonable conditions or requirements that could disadvantage employees who have an infectious disease such as Hepatitis or HIV/AIDS.

It is likely to be discriminatory for an employer to refuse to employ a person, or to terminate a person's employment because the person has an infection such as Hepatitis C or HIV/AIDS. However, there are exceptions. Under federal discrimination law and most state discrimination laws, it is not unlawful for an employer to discriminate against another person on the ground of disability if the person is unable to carry out the inherent requirements of the position. Whether an individual can carry out the inherent requirements will depend on a number of factors, including the person's past training, qualifications and experience relevant to the particular work. The inherent requirements defence only applies to certain situations in employment such as hiring and firing. For example, it does not apply in respect of an employee's access to opportunities for promotion, transfer or training.

Whether an employee with HIV/AIDS can meet the inherent requirements of a position was considered by the High Court of Australia in the case *X v. Commonwealth* (1999) 200 CLR 177. An individual employed in the army was discharged upon being diagnosed HIV positive. The Commonwealth, as his employer, argued that the individual could not be deployed as needed because, whether in training or combat, he may spill blood with the risk of transmission of HIV.

The High Court accepted that it was an inherent requirement of the employee's position that he be able to 'bleed' safely without risk of infection to others, and so the Commonwealth was found not to have unlawfully discriminated against the employee.

In addition, federal legislation permits discrimination where it is reasonably necessary to protect public health. Whether it is reasonably necessary to discriminate on the basis of a person's Hepatitis C/HIV/AIDS status in order to protect public health will depend on the circumstances of each case.

There are also obligations on employers to consider any proposal by an employee with a disability (such as having Hepatitis or HIV/AIDS) to make reasonable adjustments to allow them to perform their work. What will constitute reasonable adjustments has not yet been determined by the courts.

A person who has been refused employment or whose employment has been terminated on the basis that the person has an infection such as Hepatitis C/HIV/AIDS may lodge a complaint with the various state and federal equal opportunity/anti-discrimination tribunals and commissions. If the complaint cannot be resolved through mandatory conciliation, generally speaking, the complainant may take the matter to court.

The FW Act provides further protection for individuals with these types of infectious diseases and also makes it unlawful for an employer to terminate a person's employment on the basis of 'physical disability'. It is likely that Hepatitis C/HIV/AIDS would be regarded as a 'physical disability'.

Vilification

Certain state legislation also makes it unlawful for a person, by a public act (which includes but is not limited to any form of communication with the public, such as a newspaper article, television broadcast or a play) to incite hatred towards serious contempt for, or serious ridicule of a person or group of persons on the ground that the person or members of the group are HIV/AIDS infected or thought to be HIV/AIDS infected.

Privacy

Various state and federal legislations also prohibit employers and agencies from disclosing information regarding a person's health status in accordance with particular requirements under privacy legislation.

20.2. Checklist of Dos and Don'ts

- Employers should familiarize themselves with the National Code of Practice as a guideline for dealing with issues related to HIV/AIDS, and other similar diseases in the workplace.

- Employers should be aware of the relevant discrimination provisions in relation to disability in each state and territory in Australia in which they conduct business.
- Employers must also carefully identify the inherent requirements of a particular position. Tasks should not be too broad. To avoid claims of discrimination, employers must assess applicants on their ability to perform the inherent requirements of the position.
- An employer should assess whether the employee can perform the inherent requirements of the position, first, without assistance and second, with the provision of services which would not impose unjustifiable hardship on the employer.
- Following the reforms to the Disability Discrimination Act at the federal level, employers will also be required to consider and accommodate where possible the requests for reasonable adjustments to be made for an employee to perform a position.

21. DRESS AND GROOMING REQUIREMENTS

21.1. Overview

It is broadly accepted that employers have the right to determine dress and grooming requirements in the workplace. Equally, employers may issue a lawful and reasonable direction to an employee to abstain from wearing inappropriate or unsuitable attire at work.[6]

It is, however, unlawful to discriminate against employees on the basis of proscribed attributes, for example, age, sex, race, religion or cultural beliefs when implementing a dress or grooming policy in the workplace (*see* section 17).

When setting dress and grooming requirements, employers should ensure that the requirements are reasonable and relevant to the nature of the work to be performed. Dress requirements should be reasonable based on the appropriate presentation of corporate identity, the impact on customers or for health and safety reasons.

Employers may choose to regulate dress and grooming requirements in enterprise agreements, common law employment contracts and/or policies. A failure or refusal to comply with an employer's reasonable dress standard may result in disciplinary action being taken against the employee in accordance with the employer's policy, the contract of employment or the enterprise agreement.

---

6. For example, s. 24 of the *Equal Opportunity Act 1995* (Vic) provides that 'an employer may set and enforce standards of dress, appearance and behaviour for employees that are reasonable having regard to the nature and the circumstances of the employment'.

WHS laws are also relevant when determining appropriate dress standards in the workplace. Where workers are required to work, for example, with machinery, dangerous or hazardous substances or food, it may be necessary for workers to wear protective clothing or hygiene equipment or to refrain from wearing items such as jewellery in order to comply with health and safety legislation and associated regulations.

21.2. Checklist of Dos and Don'ts

- Dress standards and grooming requirements should be reasonable, having regard to the nature and performance of employment and the employer's corporate identity.
- Policies should be implemented uniformly to avoid allegations of discrimination.
- Unless reasonably necessary to the running of the business, policies should not limit or restrict religious or cultural attire.
- When creating dress and grooming requirements, regard should be had to relevant WHS standards.

22. PRIVACY, TECHNOLOGY AND TRANSFER OF PERSONAL DATA

22.1. Privacy Rights of Employees

In Australia, legal obligations in respect of the privacy of personal information are largely derived from statutes. There is no 'constitutional' protection of privacy rights. Privacy is regulated at both the federal and state level. Therefore, privacy obligations differ across the various jurisdictions, as well as between the public and private sectors. In each Australian jurisdiction, privacy of personal information may be regulated by specific privacy legislation and also by legislation in respect of health records, freedom of information and electronic surveillance.

A summary of some of the key legislations that regulate privacy in Australia is set out below.

Privacy Act 1988 (Cth)

The *Privacy Act 1988* (Cth) (Privacy Act) regulates the use, storage, handling, access, disclosure and security of personal information by Australian and ACT government agencies and Australian private sector organizations (including unions) with an annual turnover (i.e., gross income) greater than AUD 3 million.

There are some small businesses which may have an annual turnover of less than AUD 3 million and whose activities are regulated by the Privacy Act. These include health service providers and businesses that trade in personal information.

The Privacy Act is intended to protect 'personal information' about individuals who can reasonably be identified from the information. Personal information is generally defined as information or an opinion about an identified individual, or an individual who is reasonably identifiable, whether the information or opinion is true or not and whether the information or opinion is recorded in a material form or not.

The Privacy Act establishes thirteen Australian Privacy Principles which (together) operate to regulate the use, storage, handling, access and security of personal information by government agencies and organizations in respect of which the Privacy Act applies. Organizations may discharge their obligations by creating and complying with a Code of Practice tailored to, and approved by, the Privacy Commission for use by the organization.

The Privacy Act expressly excludes acts done, or practices engaged in, by an employer (who is regulated by the Privacy Act) or an individual, if the act or practice is directly related to a current or former employment relationship between the employer and the individual and an 'employee record' held by the organization and relating to the individual.

'Employee records' are broadly defined as a record of personal information relating to the employment of the employee. Examples of personal information relating to the employment of the employee are health information about the employee and personal information about, among other things, the engagement, training, discipline, resignation or termination of the employee; the terms and conditions of employment of the employee; the employee's personal and emergency contact details; the employee's performance or conduct; the employee's hours of employment; the employee's salary or wages; the employee's membership of a professional or trade association; and the employee's taxation, banking or superannuation affairs.

Practically, this means an employer does not need to comply with the Australian Privacy Principles (e.g., in relation to storage, access, use, and handling of the information) in relation to records about its employees which fall within the above definition.

The existence of the 'employee records' exemption does not mean that all activities of an employer that relate to employment are excluded. For example, a prospective employee does not have an employment relationship with a potential employer. Therefore, potential employers, and/or recruitment agencies must comply with the obligations of the Privacy Act in respect of candidates for employment.

Another limitation to the exemption is that it will no longer apply once an employer discloses the employee records to a third party which is not involved in the employment relationship.

Individuals must first make any complaints regarding an interference with privacy under the Privacy Act to the relevant organization (in the case of an employee, this is their employer). If the complaint is not resolved, it can be referred to the Office of the Australian Information Commissioner for investigation and conciliation, and if this is not successful, for formal determination (enforceable by the Federal Court of Australia).

If an organization has an approved Code of Practice containing complaint handling procedures, complaints must be made and steps must be taken to resolve the complaint in accordance with those procedures.

State and Territory Privacy Legislation

In most states and territories, local privacy regulation is limited to the public sector. Employers should be mindful of the following legislation which regulates the public sector:

- Victoria – *Privacy and Data Protection Act 2014* (Vic) and the *Charter of Human Rights and Responsibilities Act 2006* (Vic).
- New South Wales – *Privacy and Personal Information Protection Act 1998* (NSW).
- Queensland – *Information Privacy Act 2009* (Qld).
- Western Australia – *Freedom of Information Act 1992* (WA).
- South Australia – Information Privacy Principles (IPPs) reissued by the State Government of South Australia in 1992.
- Tasmania – Personal Information Protection Principles (*see* Schedule 1 of the *Personal Information Protection Act 2004* (Tas)).
- Northern Territory – IPPs (*see* Schedule 2 of the *Information Act 2002* (NT)).
- ACT – *Information Privacy Act 2014* (ACT) and *Human Rights Act 2004* (ACT).

There is also limited state legislation regulating privacy in respect of health records. In most states, access to health records retained by a public hospital or public health service is regulated by freedom of information legislation.

Freedom of Information Legislation

The *Freedom of Information Act 1982* (Cth) provides that every person has a right to access documents held by federal government agencies or Ministers, other than exempt documents. Relevantly, one of the classes of exempt documents is where the disclosure of the document would involve the unreasonable disclosure of 'personal information' of any person other than the applicant who has made the request. A number of factors will be taken into account in determining whether the disclosure would be 'unreasonable'.

Each state and territory also has legislation dealing with freedom of information.

Transborder Data Flow

Transborder data flow refers to the movement of personal data across national borders. The Privacy Act originally dealt only with personal information collected and handled within Australia. However, it has since been amended to apply to acts done, or practices engaged in, by an organization outside Australia and the external territories.

The Office of the Australian Information Commissioner has powers to oversee complaints that arise in respect of a breach which occurs outside of Australia, and which falls within the scope of the Privacy Act.

The purpose of these amendments to the Privacy Act was to prevent organizations from avoiding their privacy obligations by transferring the handling of personal information to countries with lower privacy protection standards.

Notifiable Data Breaches Scheme

In 2017, the Privacy Act was amended by the *Privacy Amendment (Notifiable Data Breaches) Act 2017*, which established the Notifiable Data Breaches (NDB) scheme in Australia. The NDB scheme, which commenced on 22 February 2018, applies to all agencies and organizations with existing obligations under the Privacy Act.

The NDB scheme requires notification to be given to individuals whose personal information is involved in a data breach that is likely to result in serious harm. This notification must include recommendations about the steps individuals should take in response to the breach. The Office of the Australian Information Commissioner must also be notified of eligible data breaches.

Common Law Rights to Privacy

In Australia, there is no established common law right to privacy. While the issue has been the subject of some judicial consideration, it is not yet settled law (*see Australian Broadcasting Corporation v. Lenah Game Meats Pty Ltd* [2001] HCA 63 and the Queensland District Court decision of *Grosse v. Purvis* [2003] QDC 151 as to the fact the common law in Australia is unlikely to include a right to privacy).

Workplace Surveillance

Legislation dealing with electronic surveillance (telephone, video, photographic, geographic positioning systems and computer usage) varies across states/territories and the Commonwealth. Further, the use, storage and management of information generated through surveillance will be subject to the various forms of privacy legislation discussed above.

The key legislation regulating surveillance differs in approach and regulatory effect from state to state and is as follows:

- New South Wales – *Workplace Surveillance Act 2005* (NSW) and *see also* the *Surveillance Devices Act 2007* (NSW).
- Victoria – *Surveillance Devices Act 1999* (Vic).
- Western Australia – *Surveillance Devices Act 1998* (WA).
- Queensland – there is no legislation specifically regulating workplace surveillance; however, *see Invasion of Privacy Act 1971* (QLD).
- South Australia –*Surveillance Devices Act 2016* (SA).
- Tasmania – *Listening Devices Act 1991* (Tas).
- Northern Territory – *Surveillance Devices Act 2007* (NT).
- ACT – *Listening Devices Act 1992* (ACT).
- Federal – *Telecommun*ications (Interception and Access) Act 1979 (Cth).

Workplace Searches

There is no general right in Australia (whether in common law or legislation) for an employer to search the personal property of its employees. Therefore, in order for a lawful search to be conducted, employers should obtain the consent of the employee. For example, employee belongings in an employer-owned locker should not be searched without consent.

In some cases, employers may develop policies and procedures setting out the circumstances in which an employer may seek consent to search the personal property of an employee or define areas (such as lockers) as employer property which can be accessed by an employer at any time.

However, the mere existence of a policy/procedure does not allow an employer to conduct the search. Rather, the employer may be justified in taking disciplinary action if an employee refuses the search. In all cases, the reasonableness of the employer's actions will be a relevant factor in determining what (if any) disciplinary action is appropriate. Alternatively, employers who suspect theft or misappropriation of the employer's property should consider seeking assistance from the police.

As a general rule, employers should not search for a person.

If an employer were to conduct a search without the employee's consent, the employer (or the manager who conducts the search) may be committing a criminal offence (e.g., assault, trespass or unlawful detention).

22.2. Checklist of Dos and Don'ts

- Understand the legislation regulating the collection and use of personal information as well as access to personal information.
- Do not assume regulation of privacy in Australia is the same across all jurisdictions.
- Ensure comprehensive policies and procedures are developed regulating the storage, use and disclosure of personal information.
- Train employees in the use and handling of personal information in accordance with the law.
- Do not undertake workplace surveillance until you have carefully considered the relevant legislation that applies to the state in which the relevant workplace is located.
- Have appropriate policies and procedures dealing with workplace surveillance (or email monitoring) and the management of information obtained through surveillance.
- Post signs in the workplace to inform employees of the surveillance.
- Enforce compliance with privacy policies and procedures.

23. WORKPLACE INVESTIGATIONS FOR COMPLAINTS OF DISCRIMINATION, HARASSMENT, FRAUD, THEFT AND WHISTLE-BLOWING

23.1. Overview

Specific whistle-blowing legislation requires investigations to be undertaken in certain circumstances (*see* section 16).

There is no other general legislative obligation on Australian employers to conduct an investigation of complaints of discrimination, harassment, fraud or theft. Sometimes a requirement to conduct an investigation, or the process for conducting an investigation will be set out in a company policy. Employees, clients and other stakeholders may also expect that an employer will conduct an investigation into complaints of discrimination or harassment in the workplace.

It is recommended that when such complaints are made, a thorough investigation is conducted. A thorough investigation will allow the employer to make an assessment as to whether the complaint is substantiated, the corrective action to be taken (if any) and identify whether there are any cultural or systemic issues that need to be addressed. This may prevent further complaints and litigation.

In certain circumstances, it may be appropriate for an employer to conduct an investigation at the request of its legal advisors to allow the legal advisors to provide advice. As such, legal professional privilege may attach to any documents prepared in connection with the investigation.

Failure to conduct an investigation or an inadequate investigation into a complaint may also result in the complainant commencing litigation alleging that the failure to conduct a proper investigation was a breach of the complainant's contract of employment. If the requirement to conduct an investigation in accordance with a policy is held to be a term of the contract of employment.

Employers should ensure that the conduct of any investigations is not in breach of any state or federal privacy laws or surveillance legislation (*see* section 22).

23.2. Checklist of Dos and Don'ts

During a workplace investigation, an employer should:

- Consider whether legal advice is required and consult legal advisors before creating any documents in connection with the investigation. This may assist in ensuring legal professional privilege applies to documents created during an investigation.
- Comply with all company policy documents in relation to the conduct of workplace investigations.
- Ensure that the investigation is thorough, interview appropriate persons, collect appropriate documents and follow up on additional matters raised during the course of the investigation.
- Ensure that each person involved in the investigation is aware of any confidentiality requirements in connection with the investigation.
- Do not act contrary to privacy or surveillance laws when conducting an investigation.

24. AFFIRMATIVE ACTION NON-DISCRIMINATION REQUIREMENTS

24.1. Overview

The *Workplace Gender Equality Act 2012* (Cth)(WGE Act) aims to:

- promote and improve gender equality (including equal remuneration between women and men) in employment and in the workplace;
- support employers to remove barriers to the full and equal participation of women in the workforce, in recognition of the disadvantaged position of women in relation to employment matters;

– promote, among employers, the elimination of discrimination on the basis of gender in relation to employment matters (including in relation to family and caring responsibilities);
– foster workplace consultation between employers and employees on issues concerning gender equality in employment and in the workplace;
– improve the productivity and competitiveness of Australian businesses through the advancement of gender equality in employment and in the workplace.

The WGE Act requires higher education providers and employers with over 100 employees to submit a report to the Workplace Gender Equality Agency (WGEA) between 1 April and 31 May each year for the preceding twelve-month period against a set of standardized Gender Equality Indicators (GEIs).

These GEIs include gender composition of the workforce and governing bodies; total remuneration paid to women and men during the reporting period; the availability and usage of flexible working arrangements and arrangements supporting employees with family or caring responsibilities; and the level of consultation with employees on gender equality issues within the workplace.

Employers are required to make these reports available to employees and shareholders and to notify relevant unions when the information is provided.

If an employer fails to comply with the WGE Act, the Workplace Gender Equality Agency may name the employer in a report (such as a report to the Minister or on the Agency's website) and the employer may not be eligible to compete for contracts under the Commonwealth procurement framework or eligible for Commonwealth grants or other financial assistance.

Changes which took effect on 11 April 2023 now require the WGEA to publish the gender pay gap information of relevant employers for each reporting period, with employers given the opportunity to provide a statement explaining any gender pay gap and detailing strategies that the organization is implementing to address the issue.

24.2. Checklist of Dos and Don'ts

– Employers should put in place, a programme that is aimed at eliminating discrimination and contributing to equal opportunity for women in the workplace, which deals with the matters outlined in section 24.1.
– Employers should ensure that they are aware of their reporting obligations and meet those obligations.

25. RESOLUTION OF LABOUR, DISCRIMINATION AND EMPLOYMENT DISPUTES: LITIGATION, ARBITRATION, MEDIATION AND CONCILIATION

25.1. Internal Dispute Resolution Processes

Most disputes relating to employment and labour issues in Australia are resolved through the public dispute resolution agency, the FWC, or in the Fair Work Divisions of the Federal Court of Australia and the Federal Circuit Court. Discrimination claims are handled by specialist anti-discrimination tribunals operating at both federal and state levels (*see* further section 17 of the chapter). There is only minimal use in Australia of private mediators, arbitrators and other Alternative Dispute Resolution providers for workplace disputes.

Dispute Resolution Procedures (DRPs) must be included in all modern awards and enterprise agreements made under the FW Act. These DRPs generally provide that disputes over issues arising under the award or agreement – and most entitlements under the NES – have to be resolved, initially, through a number of steps at the workplace level, for example:

- Step 1: The employee will discuss the issue/problem with his or her manager/supervisor.
- Step 2: If the dispute remains unresolved, the employee will discuss the issue/problem with a more senior management representative.

Award DRPs are required (under the FW Act) to provide that disputes which cannot be resolved through these internal processes are to be referred to the FWC for mediation, conciliation or consent arbitration (i.e., arbitration where all parties to the dispute agree to consent to arbitrate the dispute).

The model DRP for enterprise agreements (*see* Schedule 6.1, *Fair Work Regulations 2009* (Cth)) provides that disputes which cannot be resolved internally are to be referred to the FWC for mediation, conciliation or the expression of an opinion or making of a recommendation; and (if the dispute is still unresolved) the making of a binding determination (i.e., arbitration). However, parties may adopt their own DRP in an enterprise agreement, which must provide for final determination of disputes by either the FWC or another person independent of the parties (e.g., a private mediator or arbitrator). A DRP which provides for arbitration by the FWC only with the consent of the parties to the dispute will comply with this requirement.

Some employers use other internal processes for the prevention and resolution of disputes over employment and labour issues, such as open-door policies and ombudspersons (although such practices are not widespread in Australia).

25.2. Mediation and Conciliation

The FWC has a broad dispute resolution role in relation to many issues covered by the FW Act. In addition to its jurisdiction over disputes arising under the terms of modern awards, enterprise agreements, and the NES, the FWC can deal with disputes in relation to matters such as:

- enterprise agreement-making and GFB;
- union 'rights of entry' to workplaces;
- industrial action;
- general protections;
- equal remuneration;
- transfer of business.

In dealing with disputes relating to these and other matters under the FW Act, the FWC has the power to inform itself in any way it considers appropriate, including by:

- requiring a person to attend, and/or provide copies of documents, records or any other information;
- inviting oral or written submissions;
- taking evidence under oath or affirmation;
- conducting enquiries;
- undertaking or commissioning research;
- conducting conferences (usually in private), or holding hearings (usually in public);
- mediating (can be initiated by either party; each party bears its own costs; generally, there is no application fee for disputes before the FWC), conciliating, making a recommendation or expressing an opinion; and
- arbitrating, but only where this is specifically permitted by a provision of the FW Act (*see* section 25.3 below).

The FWC has also recently implemented the 'New Approaches' programme. This programme allows employers to seek assistance from the FWC to develop an alternative approach to bargaining, implementing change and resolving workplace conflict. Participation in the programme is subject to agreement, and parties can elect that the FWC provides a number of services, including:

- training in interest-based bargaining;
- facilitation of enterprise bargaining;
- facilitation of joint processes to implement enterprise agreements;
- training in interest-based dispute resolution; or
- training and facilitation in collaborative workplace change, including training for consultative committees.

25.3. ARBITRATION

The FWC may only deal with a dispute by arbitration if it is expressly authorized to do so by a provision of the FW Act. Examples of the FWC's arbitration powers under the FW Act include the following:

- the FWC may arbitrate in bargaining disputes where both parties consent;
- the FWC may make an intractable bargaining workplace determination (a form of arbitrated outcome) subsequent to an intractable bargaining declaration being made (*see* section 9.6);
- the FWC may arbitrate where protected industrial action has been ended by the FWC);
- the FWC may deal with disputes over the union's right of entry by arbitration;
- the FWC may arbitrate disputes referred to it under award or agreement DRPs (*see* section 25.1 above), where the applicable DRP empowers the FWC to do so. Rules related to the initiation of arbitration of appeal rights will generally be dealt with in the applicable DRP;
- the FWC may arbitrate a general protection matter involving a dismissal or an unlawful termination matter where both parties consent.

25.4. LITIGATION

Litigation is a frequently used method for resolving certain types of employment and labour disputes. The Fair Work Divisions of the Federal Court of Australia and the Federal Circuit Court have jurisdiction over matters arising under the FW Act (such as applications by employers to stop or prevent certain types of unlawful industrial action).

The Fair Work Divisions of the Federal Court of Australia also have jurisdiction in relation to cases where a writ of mandamus, prohibition or an injunction is sought against a person holding office under the FW Act (e.g., a member of the FWC); and appeals from the Federal Circuit Court or state or territory courts in matters arising under the FW Act.

State and territory courts have jurisdiction over disputes or other issues relating to 'common law' employment contracts (e.g., post-employment restraints and restrictions on the use of employers' confidential information); and industrial action taken outside, or in breach of, the requirements/limitations imposed by the FW Act and that may give rise to liability under the 'industrial torts'. These types of matters are also regularly litigated in the Australian Federal Court and State Supreme Courts.

A breach of a civil remedy provision gives rise to the enforcement processes set out in the FW Act. These include the ability of specified parties to bring proceedings in the Fair Work Divisions of the Federal Court of Australia or Federal Circuit Court.

Further, the *Fair Work Amendment (Protecting Vulnerable Workers) Act 2017* (Cth) amended the FW Act to impose responsibilities upon franchisors and holding companies for breaches of workplace relations laws and industrial instruments by franchisees and subsidiaries in certain circumstances:

- If a franchisor or holding company knew, or could reasonably be expected to have known, that the contravention would occur, it may be held responsible for contraventions by franchisees and subsidiaries. A franchisor or holding company may defend the matter if is it able to demonstrate that it took reasonable steps to prevent the contravention by the franchisee or subsidiary.

25.5. Fines, Penalties and Damages

Fines/penalties (pecuniary) and compensatory damages are among the remedies available in actions relating to breaches of the FW Act. The key enforcement mechanism under the FW Act is the designation of many of its provisions as 'civil remedy provisions' (e.g., obligations to comply with the NES, modern awards and enterprise agreements respectively; compliance with bargaining orders; compliance with the general protection provisions; and compliance with the provisions dealing with industrial action and right of entry).

Courts have powers to order a broad range of remedies for breaches of civil remedy provisions of the FW Act, including injunctions, compensation orders, reinstatement and civil penalties of up to AUD 16,500 (for an individual) or AUD 82,500 (for a corporation).

By reason of the *Fair Work Amendment (Protecting Vulnerable Workers) Act 2017* (Cth), penalties for a 'serious contravention' of the FW Act can result in a penalty of AUD 165,000 (for individuals) and AUD 825,000 (for a corporation). A 'serious contravention' happens when:

- the person or business knew they were contravening an obligation under workplace law;
- the contravention was part of a systematic pattern of conduct affecting one or more people.

In an action for breach of an award or enterprise agreement, for example, a court may make orders for the repayment of the amount of any underpayment that an employee has suffered; impose penalties; reinstate a dismissed employee (if appropriate); and/or issue an injunction to prevent any future breaches of the award/agreement.

These types of claims would normally be the subject of an investigation (prior to the commencement of litigation) by a Fair Work Inspector from the Office of the FWO. In addition to litigation/prosecution as a means of ensuring compliance with the FW Act and instruments made under it, the FWO can obtain 'enforceable undertakings' (i.e., undertakings given by an employer that it will stop certain conduct or a certain practice or take steps to remedy a contravention) from – or issue 'compliance notices' to – parties that have breached civil remedy provisions or awards, agreements and the like.

25.6. Checklist of Dos and Don'ts

- Employers should carefully consider the kind of DRP that will suit their operational needs when negotiating enterprise agreements (e.g., whether to provide for the reference of disputes to the FWC or a private mediator/arbitrator).
- Employers need to be familiar with the dispute resolution role and powers of the FWC and factor these into the management of employment and industrial issues at the workplace level (e.g., an awareness of the grounds/circumstances in which the FWC can arbitrate in relation to bargaining will be helpful in planning and executing negotiation strategies).
- Familiarity with the array of remedies that may be imposed for breach of the FW Act, awards, agreements, etc. – and with the investigatory powers of the FWO – may assist employers in avoiding costly and time-consuming litigation.

26. EMPLOYER RECORD-KEEPING, DATA PROTECTION AND EMPLOYEE ACCESS TO PERSONNEL FILES AND RECORDS

26.1. Overview

Record-keeping obligations are prescribed under both federal and state/territory legislation.

The FW Act and the Regulations enacted pursuant to the FW Act contain the following record-keeping obligations for employers who are subject to the FW Act:

- obligation to keep employee records, of the kind prescribed by the Regulations, for seven years; and
- those employee records must be in the form prescribed by the regulations.

26.2. Personnel Files

The Regulations require various kinds of employee records to be kept, including records regarding pay, overtime, hours of work, leave, superannuation and termination of employment. Such records must be in English and in a legible form. There is also an express obligation on an employer to ensure that employee records required to be kept under these provisions are not false or misleading, and an obligation to correct any errors in an employee record as soon as the employer becomes aware of such error.

An employer may be required to make employee records available to a Fair Work Inspector (appointed by the FWO) who is exercising 'compliance powers' under the FW Act to investigate the employment practices of an employer. A Fair Work Inspector will generally seek to inspect employee records to ascertain whether an employer is complying with the FW Act and other statutory instruments which provide minimum terms and conditions of employment. An employer must produce employee records to a Fair Work Inspector:

- upon request while a Fair Work Inspector is on the premises exercising his/her powers under the FW Act; and
- where a Fair Work Inspector has issued a notice to the employer requiring the production of employee records, in accordance with and within the time specified in such notice.

The record-keeping obligations are civil remedy provisions. Therefore a breach may result in a penalty under the FW Act. These provisions can be enforced by an employee or a Fair Work Inspector.

Under state legislation, there are similar obligations for employers to keep various kinds of employee records.

26.3. Confidentiality Rules

The Privacy Act 1988 (Cth) governs the collection, use and disclosure of personal and sensitive information by entities in the private sector. For a further discussion on privacy laws in Australia, *see* section 22.

26.4. Employee Access

Under the FW Act, an employer must make a copy of an employee record available for inspection and copying on request by the employee or former employee to whom the record relates. Similar provisions exist under state legislation relating to employee records.

27. REQUIRED NOTICES AND POSTINGS

27.1. Overview

The FW Act requires National System Employers to provide notices/information to employees in various situations, including:

- new employees – Fair Work Information Statement: From 1 January 2010, any new employee must be provided with a 'Fair Work Information Statement' prepared by the FWO. This statement is a brief document that is published on the FWO's website. This statement must be given to the employee before or as soon as possible after the employee starts work. It provides basic information about employment matters contained in the FW Act, including the NES, modern awards, enterprise agreements, workplace rights, termination of employment, union right of entry and the role of the FWO and the FWC;
- new casual employees – Casual Employment Information Statement: Every new casual employee must be provided with a 'Casual Employment Information Statement' prepared by the FWO either before or as soon as possible once they have started working for the employer. The statement explains the definition of casual employment and contains information about casual conversion. The statement covers when an employer is required to offer the conversion when an employee can request a conversion, what to do if there is a disagreement relating to conversion, and the role of the FWC;
- redundancies of fifteen or more employees: Specific notices must be issued as discussed in section 6;
- commencement of bargaining for an enterprise agreement: an employer must, except in very limited circumstances, within fourteen days of commencement of bargaining, give written notice to each employee of their right to be represented by a bargaining representative (e.g., a union) for the proposed enterprise agreement;
- withholding of pay from employees during industrial action: an employer must give employees written notice about the pay that is being withheld from employees due to the employees engaging in industrial action;
- employers must also disclose any personal financial benefits arising from enterprise agreements before they are voted on.

There is no statutory requirement for a notice board to be placed in the workplace. However, an employer and employees may make an enterprise agreement under the FW Act that contains a clause providing for a notice board. Such clause could deal with who may place notices on the board, for example, the employer, employees and/or a relevant union, the content of such notices and related issues.

Alternatively, the employer may choose to provide a notice board and could then prescribe what kinds of notices can be placed on it.

An employer should always exercise caution in relying solely upon a notice board for the purpose of providing certain notices/information to employees. In some circumstances, for example, where a particular notice must be given to individual employees, it may not be sufficient to simply post a copy of the notice on a notice board.

27.2. Checklist of Dos and Don'ts

- Obtain copies of the Fair Work Information Statement (from the FWO's website) to provide to all new employees.
- Notify Centrelink and relevant unions if fifteen or more employees' employment is to be terminated.
- Ensure you are aware of all the specific notice requirements under the FW Act in relation to bargaining for an enterprise agreement (including notice of representational rights) and industrial action.
- If there is a notice board at work, ensure all persons comply with the requirements of any applicable agreement or policy regarding what may or may not be posted on it.

www.ingramcontent.com/pod-product-compliance
Lightning Source LLC
LaVergne TN
LVHW021112300926
849160LV00009B/707
* 9 7 8 9 4 0 3 5 3 7 9 7 9 *